MODERN AIRCRAFT SERIES

Edited by Joe Christy

A new series of popular-priced books on aircraft and their operation for everyone interested in privately owned planes. Each volume is written by an expert in the field, and is printed on fine, white paper and profusely illustrated with photographs and diagrams. Each volume $1.95.

Beechcraft Guide

Parachuting for Sport

Guide to Antique Planes

Cockpit Navigation Guide

Used Plane Buying Guide

Air Traffic Control

Modern Aerobatics

Classic Bi-planes

Classic Military Biplanes

Aviation Radio for Pilots

Pilot's Weather Guide

Computer Guide

Guide to Homebuilts

Fighter Aircraft Pocketbook

Bomber Aircraft Pocketbook

Racing Planes Guide

Lightplane Engine Guide

The Piper Cub Story

Cessna Guide

Agricultural Aviation

Your Pilot's License

Instrument Flying Guide

Soaring Guide

Classic Monoplanes

Your Jet Pilot Rating

Lightplane Construction and Repair

SPORTS CAR PRESS

Distributed by CROWN PUBLISHERS
419 Park Avenue South, New York, N. Y.

Cover picture by Downie and Associates

Mike Dewey and Bob Downey round pylon at Chino, Calif., air race. Mike, on the outside, flies Foss "Jinny," modified by Jim Dewey and now known as "Little Mike." Downey's craft is Fish Salmon's #6, reworked by Irv Culver and called "Miss Cosmic Wind."

ACKNOWLEDGMENT

The author is greatly indebted to Steve Hudek for placing his fine photo collection at our disposal. Leo Kohn, who also possesses a first-rate air-photo collection, helped with pictures and moral support, as did Peter M. Bowers and Mel Stickney. And to Don Berliner, of the Professional Race Pilots Association, we offer a checkered flag attached to a gold staff and topped with a bull's head. This book surely would have foundered without his aid.

RACING PLANES GUIDE

by

JOE CHRISTY

Author of BEECHCRAFT GUIDE, YOUR PILOT'S LICENSE, *etc.*

NEW YORK

MODERN AIRCRAFT SERIES

A DIVISION OF SPORTS CAR PRESS

DEDICATION

To Art Chester and Charlie Bishop and Jim Rice and to all racing pilots, living and dead, this book is dedicated with respect and admiration. Each of these, in his own way, has paid with courage to prove all we should ever need to know about mankind in general and Americans in particular.

Library of Congress Catalog Number: 63-9457

©1963 by Sports Car Press, Ltd.

2nd Printing Dec., 1966

Published in New York by Sports Car Press, Ltd., and simultaneously in Toronto, Canada, by Ambassador Books, Ltd.

Man races because he cannot help it. He has always promoted speed contests between whatever vehicles he possessed — chariots, ocean liners and, surely there was, somewhere back there, a Brontosaurus Sweepstakes.

And it seems foolish to endow this basic, human trait with high-sounding motives. It is not true that air racing, for example, has had as its chief objective the advance of aerial technology.

It *is* true that the air races have accelerated and greatly advanced development of safe and efficient airplanes. However, improved engines and airframes have been a by-product of air racing, not its purpose.

In sum, man races airplanes because he is an adventurous, competitive, and often very courageous being — and that's reason enough.

THE WORLD'S FIRST AIR RACES were held during the week of August 22-29, 1909, on the Betheny plain near Rheims, France. This was less than six years after the Wright Brothers' first flight. A quarter-million people attended the Rheims meet, including most of the royalty of Europe.

Despite wildly-inflated prices in the nearby "Cathedral City," the spectators got their money's worth. A total of 38 aircraft were entered in the various events, and records were established daily.

During the race preliminaries, the English aeronaut, Hubert Latham, raised the world's altitude record to 508 feet; and Henri Farman kept his drafty machine aloft for over three hours to set a distance record of 118 miles.

Note: See pages 126 to 140 for chronological list of important races since 1909.

Curtiss (L) and Paulhan race at Los Angeles, 1910. (Photo: National Archives).

Curtiss pusher raced by Ruth Law had Wright Bros. control system in place of Curtiss control wheel.

Bleriot, powered with Gnome 100-hp rotary engine, was fastest plane of its day. (Photo: Institute of the Aeronautical Sciences).

THE BENNETT COUPE INTERNATIONAL was the principal event of the Rheims meet. Sponsored by James Gordon Bennett, publisher of the New York *Herald,* this contest consisted of a two-lap race around a 6.21 mile course (a total of 20 kilometers). The aeronauts did not compete simultaneously, but each took off whenever he felt that air conditions were favorable. The winner was determined by stopwatch.

Glenn H. Curtiss, piloting a Curtiss Golden Flyer, and the only American aviator present, won the race with an average speed of 47.65 mph. The great French aeronaut, Louis Bleriot, was second.

On the final day of the meet, Curtiss also won the *Prix de la Vitesse* for the fastest three laps around the course. He was lionized by all France, and his triumph hardly dimmed when the Bennett trophy presented to him featured a Wright Brothers airplane — product of his bitterest enemies.

THE FIRST AIR RACES HELD IN THE UNITED STATES were at Dominguey Field, near present-day Compton, California, January 10-20, 1910. High point of the California Aerial Exposition—though surely it was more for laughs than for thrills — was a race between a pair of one-man dirigibles. These unwieldy craft, wallowing through the air like overweight sea cows, were piloted by Roy Knabenshue and Lincoln Beachey (both of whom later became famous airplane pilots).

The outcome of this contest—as in the case of several speed matches between airplanes—was apparently considered unimportant, for there seems to be no record of the winners. However, Louis Paulhan of France did raise the world's altitude record to a breath-taking 4,165 feet.

THE LONDON-MANCHESTER RACE, sponsored by the London Daily Mail, was held in April, 1910. Fifty thousand dollars was offered to the first aeronaut to fly between London and Manchester—a distance of 183 miles—within 24 hours. Claude Grahame-White of England and Louis Paulhan of France took off on the morning of the 27th. Both landed short of their goal and spent the night in Lichfield. The English aeronaut was first into the air next morning but was soon forced down with engine trouble. Paulhan won the prize with a flying time of 5 hours and 15 minutes.

A CIRCUIT OF GERMANY RACE was held in May, 1910 (the first airplane to be built in Germany had flown only the year before) for a 50,000-mark purse. German Aeronauts Obering and Hirth, flying an Etrich *Taube,* were the winners. Herr Volmoller, also in a *Taube,* placed second.

ENGLAND'S BOURNEMOUTH AERIAL TOURNAMENT, held July 10-16, 1910, ended on a tragic note. Hon. Charles S. Rolls, of Rolls-Royce fame, crashed to his death in his flimsy plane. Leon Morane won the feature race around the Isle of Wight.

THE HARVARD-BOSTON AIR MEET offered ten days of stunting, record attempts and air racing. Site of the meet was Boston Harbor, and the date, September 3-13. The Boston *Globe* put up a $10,-000 purse for the fastest round trip between Boston Light and Sqantum, and England's Grahame-White barely nosed out Glenn Curtiss to win with an average speed of 58 mph. The English flier's machine was a Farman biplane.

THE 1910 BENNETT CUP RACE was the feature attraction of a grand aerial exposition held at Belmont Park, L. I. in October. This affair was the U. S. answer to the Rheims meet of the year before. The United States had no royalty, but there were plenty of self-made millionaires on hand—and some decorative actresses —and so the total effect was about the same. According to newspapers of the day, this meet was the top society sporting event of the decade.

Forty airplanes were entered, and again records were shattered. Ralph Johnstone upped the altitude mark to 9,714 feet (an hour and forty-three minutes were required for him to reach this unheard-of height), and Alfred Leblanc of France achieved a top speed of 70 mph in a Bleriot monoplane.

The Bennett Cup race turned into a thriller, and Claude Grahame-White was hard pressed to beat out such aeronauts as America's John B. Moisant, flying a Bleriot, Hubert Latham, piloting an Antoinette, Alec Ogilvie in a Wright Model C and Walter Brookin's Wright Model R (Baby Wright). The winning plane was a Bleriot, and Grahame-White's average speed was 61 mph for the 62-mile course. Moisant was second; Ogilvie third.

French Nieuport racer of 1911 was world's fastest plane at 90 mph.
(Photo: French Embassy).

1912 Deperdussin was first airplane to exceed 100 mph. (Photo:
National Archives).

Avro Arrowscout rounds pylon in 1914 Olympic Air Race. (Photo:
Avro).

Famed WW I DH-4 doubled as a racer in many air meets of the twenties. (Photo: Steve Hudek).

Casey Jones flew a Curtiss Jenny to second place in 1919 New York-Toronto race. His reward was a free meal and a wrist watch. (Photo: George Pollard).

Capt. Maxwell Kirby flew this SE-5 to 14th place in 1920 Pulitzer race. (Photo: U.S.A.F.).

THE STATUE OF LIBERTY RACE was an added attraction of the Belmont meet. It was sponsored by New York Industrialist T. F. Ryan, who offered $10,000 to the winner of a race around this proud symbol of freedom and back to Belmont. Moisant was first across the finish line but was disqualified, and the purse went to France's Count Jaques de Lesseps.

At Belmont, the girls began to appear as pilots for the first time. Mlle. Helene Dutrieux drew gasps from the crowds as she put her Bleriot through its paces. She was not allowed to compete with the men, although, back in her own country a little later, Helene won the *Coupe Femina* with an average speed of 40 mph. Other early "aviatrices," as they were called, were Americans Blanche Scott, Ruth Law, Harriet Quimby (the "Dresden China Doll"), and Mathilde Moisant. Katherine and Marjorie Stinson followed in 1912.

Most of the early racing and exhibition fliers worked for the aircraft manufacturers because, despite the generous prizes offered at the various meets prior to WW I, few individuals could afford to equip themselves with a flying machine, spare parts, mechanics, etc., and then transport this equippage and personnel between hemispheres in quest of the fat purses.

Company aeronauts received an average of $20 per week, plus $50 for each flight. In addition, each was compensated for travel and living expenses while away from home. All prize money went to the sponsoring company.

It was a dangerous business. During 1910 alone, 37 professional fliers were killed while racing or stunting.

THE BENNETT CUP RACE OF 1911 took place on Saturday, July 1, at Eastchurch, England. As in most international competitions, the country in possession of the trophy played host. English entries were Alec Ogilvie flying a Wright Model R, and Gustav Hamel in a Bleriot. French contestants were Chevalier, piloting a Nieuport; Edouard Nieuport, in one of his own creations, and Alfred Leblanc, flying a Bleriot monoplane. The single U. S. entry was Charles Weymann, equipped with one of the new streamlined Nieuports. This year, the race consisted of 25 laps around a 3.75-mile course for a total distance of 94 miles.

Pre-race tests had convinced Hamel that the Nieuports were faster than his Bleriot; so, anticipating the Thompson racers of

Breguet XIX, racer prototype of first plane to fly westbound non-stop from Paris to New York. (Photo: U.S.A.F.)

Fairey III racing seaplane built for Schneider Cup race of 1920. (Fairey Aviation Co. Photo).

Sopwith 107 "Rainbow," British racer of the early twenties. (Photo: Hawker Aircraft Co.).

Nieuport-Delage 29, winner of 1920 Bennett Cup race. (Photo: U.S.A.F.).

U.S. Army Verville VCP-R, 1920 Bennett Cup entry flown by "Shorty" Schroeder. (Photo: U.S.A.F.).

Dayton-Wright racer (Baumman RB-1), 1920 Bennett entry, featured retractable landing gear and cantilever wing. (Photo: U.S.A.F.).

almost four decades later, Hamel chopped a couple of feet off his wingtips to gain speed. He went into a high-speed stall at the first pylon, but he was not seriously injured.

Weymann placed first with an average of 78 mph, thus returning the Cup to the United States. Leblanc was second with a 75.8 and Nieuport third with 75.1 mph.

THE CHICAGO AVIATION MEET OF 1911, held in August, was notable for a risky race over Lake Michigan. It resulted in the world's first air-sea rescue. When Rene Simon fell into the water with a dead engine, Hugh Robinson, flying Glenn Curtiss' new hydroplane, landed alongside the wreck and pulled Simon aboard.

Other races during the summer and fall of 1911 included THE PARIS TO MADRID RACE, which was won by Jules Vedrines of France; the CIRCUIT OF ENGLAND RACE, won by Lt. Jean Conneau of France, and a repeat of the Boston *Globe's* cross-country event that England's Grahame-White had won the year before.

THE SQUANTUM AIR MEET featured this latter contest in September. The course was from Boston to Nashua, N. H., then to Worcester, Mass., on to Providence, R. I., and back to Boston. There were four entries: Earle Ovington, flying a Bleriot; Harry Atwood in a Burgess-Wright; Lt. T. D. Milling, piloting a Wright biplane and Arthur Stone at the controls of a Queen Monoplane (the Queen was an American-made Bleriot). Ovington collected the $10,000 first prize by outlasting the others.

THE FIRST TRANSCONTINENTAL FLIGHT lasted from September 17 to December 10, 1911, and was made by Calbraith P. Rodgers. It was a race in the sense that William Randolph Hearst's $50,000-prize offer stipulated that the winner must complete an ocean-to-ocean flight within 30 days. Rodgers didn't win, and he cracked up so many times that only the rudder and one strut of his original plane, the "Vin Fizz," completed the trip, but he gained lasting fame for his courage and refusal to give up. Rodgers' actual flying time totaled 82.4 hours for the 4,251 miles.

THE BENNETT CUP RACE OF 1912, held September 9 at Chicago, emphasized France's aerial superiority. Although the airplane had been invented in the United States, it was the French who

Navy Loening M-8, 1920 Pulitzer entry. (Photo: U.S.A.F.).

Lt. Corliss Moseley and his Verville VCP-R racer, winner of 1920 Pulitzer Cup race.

Ansaldo "Balilla" flown by Bert Acosta; third in 1920 Pulitzer race. (Photo: Fiat Aircraft Co.).

16

Army Thomas-Morse MB-3 flown by Maj. Hartney to 2nd place in 1920 Pulitzer race. (Photo: Steve Hudek).

Navy Curtiss 18-T-1 triplane racer. Two entered in 1920 Pulitzer —both dropped out with engine trouble. (Photo: U. S. Navy). (Hudek Collection).

French Spad racer developed from famous WW I fighter. (Photo: Steve Hudek)

did most to develop it during the years preceding WW I. And at Chicago they showed up with a pair of Deperdussin monoplanes so advanced in design that everyone else chickened-out.

With no competition, the three-man French team had to compete among themselves for the trophy: Maurice Prevost and Jules Vedrines in the Deperdussins, and Andre Frey in a new Hanroit. Vedrines sped around the 30-lap 124.8-mile course in a little over an hour to average 105.5 mph. During the race, he also established a new world's speed record for 20 kilometers at 107 mph. Prevost was second with 103.8 mph, and Frey dropped out with engine trouble.

THE FIRST SCHNEIDER TROPHY RACE, April 6, 1913, took place at Monaco (Princess Grace's fiefdom today) on the French Riviera. This international contest for seaplanes was conceived by Jacques Schneider, a wealthy French aviation enthusiast, who believed that development of hydroplanes was being neglected. He offered a yearly prize of about $5,000 cash, plus a trophy of equal value, to the winner of a 174-mile race over open water. Permanent possession of the trophy would go to any country winning it three years in a row. The prize money was, of course, little more than a token; but with the issue of national prestige involved, several Western countries eventually invested heavily in an effort to win the Schneider.

Three French pilots and one American entered the 1913 race; Prevost, in a float version of his record-breaking Deperdussin; Roland Garros (later a famed war ace), in a Morane-Saulnier; Espanet in a Nieuport and the American, Charles Weymann, also in a Nieuport. All four planes were powered with the 160-hp twin-row Gnome rotary engine.

Garros and Espanet dropped out of the race with engine trouble soon after take off, leaving Weymann and Prevost to battle it out. Weymann was leading at the 124-mile mark when his engine's rear-bank of cylinders became overheated—a common source of trouble with the twin-row Gnomes and he was forced down. Prevost completed the race, though his average speed was cut to 45.8 mph when the judges required that he re-fly part of the last lap. However, Prevost would have won at any speed he turned in, for he was the only contestant still flying.

18

Spad racer flown to second place in 1920 Bennett by Bernard de Romanet. (Photo: U.S.A.F.). (Hudek Collection).

Curtiss-Cox "Texas Wildcat"—before 1920 Bennett race. (Photo: Curtiss-Wright). (Hudek Collection).

Curtiss-Cox "Texas Wildcat"—after 1920 Bennett race. (Photo: Curtiss-Wright). (Hudek Collection)

THE BENNETT CUP RACE OF 1913 was held on Monday, September 29, at Rheims, France. The altitude record went up to 19,033 feet, and the speed record was broken again. England, Germany, and the United States withdrew from the race, apparently because they had nothing to match the performance of the French entries. Belgium did enter, though Crombez, the Belgian pilot, was flying a French Deperdussin. The French team consisted of Prevost and Gilbert, also in Deperdussins, and Emile Vedrines (no relation to Jules Vedrines) in a Ponnier. The Ponnier, as the Hanriot, was a copy of the Nieuport racer.

The race was 20 laps around a 6.21-mile course. Prevost, who had clipped the wings of his Deperdussin, flew a daring race, diving around pylons and brushing tree tops. He placed first, with an average speed of 124.5 mph. Vedrines, crowding the leader all the way, was second with 123 mph. Gilbert was third at 119.5 mph, and Crombez last.

THE LONDON DAILY MAIL AERIAL DERBY, a little-known race over a 95-mile course, took place on September 20, 1913. The winner was Gustav Hamel, flying a Bleriot monoplane. Hamel was later to disappear on May 23, 1914 on a flight over the English Channel.

THE SCHNEIDER TROPHY RACE OF 1914, again at Monaco, was flown on Monday, April 20. There were nine entries: three French, two British, two Americans (Weymann and Thaw), one German and one Swiss. However, only five planes actually started the race, which was 28 laps around a 10-kilometer course.

One of the English pilots, C. H. Pixton, was equipped with a Sopwith Tabloid; although this was a biplane design, it was very clean aerodynamically and handled well on the water. This latter characteristic paid off because of a special rule this year which required that each contestant make two water landings and take offs, at specified points, during the race.

Pixton won with an average of 86.8 mph; after taking the checkered flag he opened his throttle for two additional laps and established a new speed record for seaplanes at 92 mph. The second English pilot, Lord Carberry, was unable to get back into the air after his first water landing. Frenchmen Espanet and Levasseur were forced down with engine trouble in mid-race.

Curtiss-Cox "Cactus Kitten" 1920 Bennett entry piloted by Roland Rohlfs, famous earlybird. (Curtiss-Wright Photo).

Gloster "Bamel," winner of 1921 and 1922 British Aerial Derby, evolved into the Gloster racers of Schneider Cup fame. (Photo: Gloster).

Bert Acosta, winner of 1921 Pulitzer race, and his Navy Curtiss CR-1. (Curtiss Photo).

Clarence Coombs and his Curtiss-Cox "Cactus Kitten" (converted from monoplane). Second place in 1921 Pulitzer. (Curtiss Photo).

Lt. John A. McReady walked away from the crash of this Army Thomas-Morse R-2 racer during 1921 Pulitzer at Omaha. (U.S.A.F. Photo).

Major Hartney crashed this Thomas-Morse R-5 racer during 1921 Pulitzer. Coolant radiator is slung between landing gear on this all-metal plane. (U.S.A.F. Photo).

Nieuport-Delage racer won 1922 Coupe Deutsch de la Meurthe at Etampes, France. In 1923 it took world's landplane speed record at 234.66 mph. (U.S.A.F. Photo).

Grover Loening (R) and Loening R-4, 1922 Pulitzer entry. (U.S.A.F. Photo).

Nieuport-Delage experimental racer. Coolant radiator between wheels. (U.S.A.F. Photo).

Their Neiuports were powered with the twin-row Gnome rotaries and the rear cylinders overheated.

Burri, the Swiss, piloting an F.B.A. Flying Boat, straggled in to take second place after stopping to refuel. The only two planes to finish were powered with single-row Gnome engines of 100 hp. And the greater dependability of this smaller engine, as proven in the prewar Schneider and Bennett races, was probably the reason that WW I designers chose it over the more powerful twin-row Gnome.

About this time, Armand Deperdussin, whose company was building the most advanced airplanes of the day, went to jail on charges of stock-swindling. Louis Bleriot took over the Deperdussin works and renamed it the *Societe Pour Aviation et Derives* (S.P.A.D.). Late in WW I the same young engineer that had designed the Deperdussin monoplane, Louis Bechereau, came up with a biplane design that is remembered today as one of the allies' best fighter planes—the Spad.

THE SCHNEIDER TROPHY RACE of 1919 took place on April 20, at Bournemouth, England. Italy had, during the late war, spent much developing flying boats and showed up with the fastest plane, a Savoia S-13. The race, however, was flown in a dense fog and everyone got lost except the Italian pilot, Janello. He completed the course and landed, but due to protests from some of the others charging that he had circled some of the harbor buoys rather than the official pylons, race judges finally declared the 1919 Schneider competition no contest.

THE NEW YORK—TORONTO RACE, held August 25, 1919, was billed as the world's first international air race. It was inspired by inauguration of air mail service between the United States and Canada. The race consisted of a round trip between New York and Toronto, with several specified fuel stops enroute. Contestants were allowed to start from either end. Seventeen Canadian entries took off from Toronto, and eleven Americans from New York. Most of the planes were WW I surplus DH-4's, Curtiss Jennies and SE-5's, although three Americans—Roland Rolphs, Bert Acosta and J. D. Hill—piloted new Curtiss Orioles.

Two starting points, and two finish lines, made for a lot of confusion, and it was several days before the race committee announced the winners. Many planes did not complete the race, and at least two disappeared — apparently into Lake Ontario. Roland Rolphs was declared the winner; Casey Jones (flying a Curtiss Jenny) placed second, and S. S. Moore was third. However, according to Casey Jones (writing in a recent issue of the *American Historical Society Journal*), no one ever collected any of the $10,000 prize money offered by a New York hotel. His share of the purse, he says, was a free meal and a Waltham watch.

THE SCHNEIDER TROPHY RACE OF 1920 was hosted by Venice, Italy, on September 22. The 222-mile course—10 laps around a 22.2-mile triangle — just outside Venice Lagoon, saw no entries, however, except Italians. And of these, only Lt. Luigi Bologna was able to qualify. Flying a Sovoia S-12, powered with a 500-hp Ansaldo engine, he sped around the course at an average speed of 107.2 mph and was declared the winner.

THE BENNETT CUP RACE of 1920 attracted some interesting new designs. An American entry, the Dayton-Wright racer RB-1, sported the world's first retractable landing gear, had a cantilever wing, and was exceptionally-well streamlined.

Two other U.S. entries, built by Curtis for Texas Oilman S.E.J. Cox, were the 'Texas Wildcat," a biplane with enclosed cockpit and powered with a Curtiss D-12 engine of 435 hp; and the "Cactus Kitten," identical to the Wildcat except that it was a high-wing monoplane. The other U.S. entry was an Army Air Service Verville biplane, VCP-1, which had a Packard V-12 engine of 638 hp swinging its prop.

The race was held on September 28 at Villesauvage Airdrome near Etampes, France. The Texas Wildcat was damaged in a landing accident before the race began (Pilot Roland Rolphs was uninjured), and the Cactus Kitten was not risked because of its high landing speed and the small field available to the racers.

This was before the day of the 'race-horse start" in air racing, and the participants took off one at a time, with the winner determined by stopwatch. France's Kirch, flying a Nieuport 29, was off first followed by Bernard de Romanet in a new Spad racer and Sadi-Lecointe in another Nieuport. Next was Howard Rinehart in the Dayton-Wright, then Maj. "Shorty" Schroeder

Lt. Lester Maitland captured 2nd in 1922 Pulitzer with this Army
Curtiss R-6 racer powered with Curtiss D-12 engine. His speed was
198.8 mph. (U.S.A.F. Photo).

Lt. Maughan took 1st in 1922 Pulitzer flying this Curtiss R-6 racer.
Later, Gen. Billy Mitchell established new landplane speed record
in this craft. (U.S.A.F. Photo).

Booth & Thurston BR-1 (Bee-line Special), one of pair built for U.S.
Navy. Entered in 1922 Pulitzer, these craft had retractable gears and
flush wing-radiators. (U.S.A.F. Photo).

Army Verville-Sperry R-3 racer flown by Lt. Barksdale in 1922 Pulitzer, was clean design with retractable gear. (U.S.A.F. Photo).

Retractable landing gears sometimes created problems in 1922. Forty years later they still do. (U.S.A.F. Photo).

Thomas-Morse MB-7, built for Army and borrowed by Marine Corps for 1922 Pulitzer race. (U.S.A.F. Photo).

flying the Verville-Packard. Last man off was Raynham of England, in a Martinsyde Semiquaver.

Kirch was forced down with engine trouble at the end of the first lap. Rinehart, in the radical Dayton-Wright, did not even complete a single circuit before he dropped out with a broken rudder cable. Then the U.S.'s final hope was dashed when the Verville-Packard was forced to pull out with an overheated engine — and the first lap also accounted for England's single entry when Raynham quit with a broken oil line. The two Frenchmen were left to battle it out, and Sadi-Lecointe outlasted his countryman to bring the Nieuport 29 across the finish line with an average of 168.5 mph. De Romanet averaged 113.5 mph to take second, despite having to land and repair his plane during the race.

France's third win in a row earned her permanent possession of the Bennett Cup.

THE FIRST PULITZER TROPHY RACE was held on Thanksgiving Day, November 27, 1920, at Mitchel Field, Long Island. This trophy was sponsored by Ralph Pulitzer (what would early air racing have done without newspaper publishers?), who sought to establish a new international unlimited speed event.

The course was a triangle—Mitchel Field to Lufberry Field to Henry Damm Field—totalling 29.02 miles. The race consisted of four laps around this course for a total of 116.08 miles. The only restriction imposed upon participating aircraft was that none should have a landing speed in excess of 75 mph. As in the Bennett and the Schneider races, the pilots took off one after another and were timed separately. Thirty seven planes started; 25 finished. Most were military.

Capt. Corliss Mosely, flying the same Verville-Packard that had made but one lap in the Bennett two months before, solved his engine-cooling problem and took first place with an average of 156.5 mph. Mosely was actually in second place until a sleek new Loening Navy racer, averaging almost 160 mph, was forced down just a mile short of the finish line with a broken water connection.

Second place went to Harold Hartney, famous WW I ace, flying a Thomas-Morse MB-3, powered with a 300 hp Hisso. His speed was 148 mph. Civilian Bert Acosta, in an Italian Ansaldo

Supermarine Sea Lion III, flown by Capt. Baird, won the Schneider Trophy for England in 1922. Rear cockpit was covered for race. (Supermarine Photo).

Navy-Wright "Mystery" racer was a 1922 Pulitzer entry. (U.S.A.F. Photo).

Army Verville-Packard Special. (U.S.A.F. Photo).

Lt. Al Williams, winner of 1923 Pulitzer, and his Navy Curtiss R2C-1 racer. (Navy Photo).

Navy Lt. Harold Brow and Curtiss CR-2, second in 1923 Pulitzer at 241.8 mph. (Navy Photo).

Navy-Wright F2W racer. 1923 Pulitzer entry. (Navy Photo).

Balilla, was third. A DeHavilland DH-4—one of 13 entered—took sixth place at 124 mph. Two Navy Curtiss triplanes dropped out with engine trouble.

THE SCHNEIDER TROPHY RACE of 1921, again at Venice and over the same course, saw one Frenchman join the ten Italian entries. All the Italian planes were military flying boats. The French hopeful was equipped with a Nieuport floatplane—but he banged-up his floats during pre-race tests, leaving the field to the Italians once again.

In accordance with Schneider race rules, which stipulated that no country could enter more than three airplanes, elimination trials weeded out seven Italians. Thus the race, flown on August 11, was between three Italian flying boats. Lt. Zanetti, in a two-place Macchi M-19 powered with a 720-hp Fiat V-12 engine, landed on the water when his plane caught fire. He and his mechanic got out safely. Then Lt. Corniglio, flying a Macchi M-7, ran out of gas. This left only de Briganti, piloting another Macchi M-7 (powered with a 250-hp V-12 Isotta engine), to go on and win if he could merely stay in the air long enough. He did. His average speed was 117.9 mph.

THE PULITZER TROPHY RACE of 1921 was staged at Omaha, Neb., on November 3. It consisted of 5 laps around a 31.07-mile triangular course. Bert Acosta, now a Curtiss test pilot, entered a new Curtiss Navy racer equipped with a Curtiss CD-12 engine of 405 hp. Clarence Coombs would pilot the Cactus Kitten, which had gone to France the year before as a Bennett entry but had not flown. The Kitten was now a triplane—a circumstance decreed by the 75-mph landing speed limit placed on all Pulitzer entries. James Curran entered an Italian SVA-9, and Lloyd Bertaud an Ansaldo Balilla, also an Italian design. Other contestants were J.A. Macready in a Thomas-Morse MB-6, and Harold Hartney (the war ace), in a Thomas-Morse MB-7.

Acosta won with an average speed of 176.7 mph, after a tough battle with the Cactus Kitten. Apparently, the Kitten was the faster plane, but Coombs was new to it and lost precious ground during the early laps before he became accustomed to its handling characteristics. He placed second with an average speed of 170.3 mph. Macready copped third with 160.7 mph. Hartney

The end of the Navy F2W racer #7 at St. Louis, Mo., Pulitzer race of 1923. (U.S.A.F. Photo).

Navy Lt. Dave Rittenhouse won the Schneider Trophy for the U.S. in 1923, flying this Curtiss CR-3. (Navy Photo).

Gloster II racer, built for the 1923 Schneider, was damaged in trials and did not participate. (Gloster Photo).

crash-landed on the first lap as a result of sudden fuel pump failure.

THE SCHNEIDER TROPHY RACE of 1922 climaxed a week-long aviation meet held at Naples, Italy. Four planes—all single-engine flying boats — were entered. Three of these were Italian; the fourth, English. And, for once, everybody finished. Capt. H. C. Baird, flying a Supermarine Sea Lion III, took first place in a close contest with Italy's Passaleva piloting a Savoia S-51. Their speeds were 145.7 mph and 143.5 mph respectively. Zanetti was third with 133 mph in a Macchi M-17, and Cornolino last with a 90.6-mph average in a Macchi M-7. The race was 13 laps around a triangular course for a total of 230.3 miles. It was flown on August 13.

THE PULITZER TROPHY RACE of 1922 took place at Detroit on October 14. Required were 5 laps around a 31.07-mile circuit for a total of 155.35 miles. It ran from Selfridge Field to Mount Clemens to Gaukler Point to a sausage balloon anchored in Lake St. Clair, then back to Selfridge Field.

Three Verville-Sperrys, flown by Army Lts. Barksdale, Johnson, and Capt. St. Clair Streett, and a Navy Bee-Line Special, piloted by Lt. Callaway, were low-wing monoplanes featuring retractable landing gears. All four of these racers were powered with the 380-hp liquid-cooled Wright H-3 engine.

Other entries were a Thomas-Morse MB-7 flown by Navy Capt. Mulcahy; a Navy "Mystery" ship piloted by Lt. Sanderson, which was an unusual sesquiplane design powered with a 650-hp Packard T-2 engine; Capt. Mosely, in the Verville-Packard biplane (winner of the 1920 Pulitzer); two new low-wing Loening racers, flown by Army Lts. Whitehead and Schultz; a pair of Army Thomas-Morse TM-22 parasol monoplanes flown by Capt. Hunter and Lt. Bissell, plus four of the sleekest biplanes built up to that time: the new Curtiss Racers.

Two of these were entered by the Navy and piloted by Lts. Brow and Al Williams; the other two were Army entries, flown by Lts. Maughan and Maitland. These craft were powered with Curtiss D-12 engines of 460 hp. Chief distinguishing feature between the Navy and Army Curtiss Racers was N-type wing struts on the Navy jobs; I-type interplane struts were used in the

Navy-Wright NW-2 racer, flown by Lt. Wead, was scratched from 1923 Schneider because of pre-race accident. (Wright Photo).

Army Lt. Harry Mills piloted this slicked-up Verville-Sperry R-3 to victory in the 1924 Pulitzer race. (U.S.A.F. Photo).

Army Lt. Alex Pearson died in this Curtiss R-8, a 1924 Pulitzer entry. Note fabric-covered wheels for stream-lining. (U.S.A.F. Photo).

Army Lt. Stoner flew this Curtiss PW-8A, a standard Pursuit plane, to 3rd place in 1924 Pulitzer. (U.S.A.F. Photo).

Warrant Officer Bonnet of the French Air Force set new landplane speed record of 278.48 mph in this Ferbois-Bernard racer in 1924. Record stood until 1932. (Photo: Union Syndicate des Industries Aeronautiques).

Lt. Cy Bettis won 1925 Pulitzer in this Curtiss R3C-1. (U.S.A.F. Photo).

Army design. All incorporated corrugated-brass wing-covering as radiators.

These four Curtiss Racers claimed the first four places. Lt. Maughan was first, averaging 205.8 mph. Lt. Maitland took second money with 198.8, and Lt. Brow third with 193.2 mph. Al Williams was fourth with an average speed of 188. Lt. Sanderson plopped the Navy Mystery ship into Lake St. Clair when it developed engine trouble. He swam ashore uninjured. Lt. Barksdale was fifth; Mosely sixth.

Four days later, General Billy Mitchell, the Father of American Airpower, flew the winning Curtiss Racer over a 3-kilometer course four times for an average of 224.4 mph and a new world's speed record.

THE FIRST JOHN L. MITCHELL TROPHY RACE, sponsored by General Mitchell in honor of his brother who had died in WW I, was flown on the same day as the Pulitzer. Limited to the First Pursuit Group (stationed at Selfridge Field), the contest consisted of four laps around the 31.07-mile Pulitzer course. All entries flew identical Thomas-Morse MB-3's. Lt. Stace was the winner with an average of 148-mph.

THE SCHNEIDER TROPHY RACE of 1923 was hosted by England on September 28. The course was five times around a triangle—Cowes-Selsey-Southsea—measuring 42.86 miles for a total of 214 miles. U.S. entries were three Navy planes. Two of these were float versions of the Curtiss Racers that had swept the Pulitzer the year before, and were flown by Lts. David Rittenhouse and Rutledge Irvine. The third Navy entry was a Wright NW-2, piloted by Lt. A. W. Gorton. Accompanying this team was Lt. Frank Wead with a Navy TR-3 biplane, intended as an alternate.

The British team lost two of its entries to pre-race accidents and had, as a starter, only H. C. Baird in the Supermarine Sea Lion III (winner of the 1922 Schneider). France sent three planes, plus an alternate, but only one, a CAMS-38 flown by Hurel, participated.

The Curtiss Racers left no doubt of their superior design when Lts. Rittenhouse and Irvine easily romped in first and second with speeds of 177.4-mph and 173.5-mph. England's Baird was third at 157.2; his increase in speed over the previous year was

1925 Schneider Trophy went to Jimmy Doolittle flying this Curtiss R3C-2. Speed: 232.6 mph. (Curtiss Photo).

Italian Macchi M-33 was third in 1925 Schneider race. (Macchi Photo).

Gloster III, flown to 2nd place in 1925 Schneider race by Capt. Broad of the Royal Flying Corps.

Curtiss P-1 "Hawk," standard Air Corps fighter, participated in '25, '26 and 1927 Pulitzer races.

Curtiss "Oriole" in which Casey Jones averaged 134.2 mph in civilian free-for-all at 1925 National Air Races. (Ford Mtr. Co. Photo).

Curtiss P-1 Hawk racer with inverted air-cooled Liberty engine; disqualified for pylon-cutting in 1926 Nationals. (U.S.A.F. Photo).

due to a new Napier engine of 575 hp. The French CAMS-38 dropped out in the second lap. The American NW-2 had been eliminated several days before when a broken prop gashed a float; and the Navy TR-3 alternate did not start because of a balky engine.

THE PULITZER TROPHY RACE of 1923 was a feature of the St. Louis Air Meet—probably the largest air meet in the world up to that time. Race day was October 6, and seven planes competed. Lt. Alford Williams placed first and Lt. H. J. Brow was second. Their speeds were 243.7-mph and 241.8-mph. Their planes were a pair of new Navy Curtiss R2C-1's, slicked-up versions of the Curtiss Racers that had beaten everything in sight.

Other participants were two Navy Wright F2W racers that much resembled the Curtisses. And although the F2W's had 700-hp engines, against only 500-hp D-12's in the R2C-1's, the F2W's flown by Lts. Callaway and Sanderson, proved slower. Saunderson's fastest lap was 240.3 mph (he averaged 230.1—then crashed into a haystack with empty gas tanks just after crossing the finish line).

Army entries were a pair of Curtiss Racers piloted by Lts. Corkhill and Miller, and a Verville-Sperry R-3 flown by Lt. Pearson. Corkhill's speed was 216.5 mph; and Lt. Pearson was forced out with an unbalanced prop spinner. The Curtiss Racer flown by Lt. Miller was the one in which Lt. Maughan had won last year's Pulitzer, but it finished out of the money. The winning speed had been upped 37 mph over last year's figure.

Later that year, Lt. Al Williams established a new speed mark of 266.6 mph in the F2C-1.

THE SCHNEIDER TROPHY RACE was not held in 1924 — possibly because no other country had anything to match the U.S. Navy's Curtiss R2C's. (Equipped with floats, called R3C).

THE NATIONAL AIR RACES of 1924 were at Dayton, Ohio, October 2-4. Several races were limited to civilian airplanes, although the two biggest events—that is, the speediest ones—were the John L. Mitchell Trophy Race and the Pulitzer, and these were military shows.

THE MITCHELL TROPHY RACE was a thrilling one for the spectators

Navy-Wright "Apache" racer, entered in 1926 Pulitzer. (U.S.A.F. Photo).

Lt. Tom Tomlinson piloted this Curtiss F6C-3 to 4th in the 1926 Schneider. This plane was later converted to Marine Capt. Page's XF6C-6. (U.S. Navy Photo).

Italian Maj. Mario de Bernardi and his first-place Macchi M-39 which won 1926 Schneider at 246.49 mph. (Macchi Photo).

because the First Pursuit Group was equipped with new Curtiss PW-8's, a fighter plane directly developed from the Curtiss Racers, and powered with the same 460-hp D-12 engine; and because a diving start, culminating immediately before the grand-stands, marked the beginning of the contest. The 11 entries flew the same course as the Pulitzer contestants, which was 4 laps around the 31.07-mile course for a total of 124.28 miles.

Lt. Cy Bettis, who led the starting dive, maintained his front-running position throughout the race and won with a speed of 175.5 mph. However, the planes and pilots were so evenly matched that there was but an eleven-mph spread between first and last place—the eleventh-place speed was 164.2—and only .4 mph between second and third. Second-place winner was Lt. Stace with 173.7, and third went to Lt. Matthews at 173.3-mph.

THE PULITZER TROPHY RACE attracted but four planes this year. All were Army planes: a pair of Curtiss R-6 racers, flown by Capt. Burt Skeel and Lt. Brookley; a Curtiss PW-8A Pursuit piloted by Lt. Rex Stoner, and the Verville-Sperry which had dropped out of the 1923 race, piloted now by Lt. H. H. Mills.

Again the diving start was allowed—and this time it brought tragedy. Capt. Skeel's R-6 shed its wings and the fuselage buried itself 10 feet into the muck of a stream bank.

The others, of course, continued, and Lt. Mills flew the Verville-Sperry to victory at 215.7 mph. Lt. Brookley, in the remaining R-6 crowded Mills all the way and placed second with 214.8 mph. Lt. Stoner, in the PW-8A, finished way back with a speed of 168 mph.

THE NATIONAL AIR RACES of 1925 were held at Mitchel Field, L.I., October 8-13. More than 160 planes participated in the various events; three-fourths of the aircraft present were civilian.

THE MITCHELL TROPHY RACE was, as usual, a close one. Ten Curtiss PW-8's were entered by the First Pursuit Group. Lt. T .K. Matthews placed first with an average of 161.5-mph. Lt. Schulgen was second with 158.7-mph. The slower speeds were due to discontinuance of the diving start (because of the death of Capt. Skeel the year before), and a course shortened to only 12 miles around and requiring tighter turns.

THE PULITZER TROPHY RACE consisted of the usual 4 laps around

41

1927 Schneider entry, England's Gloster IV, was fastest biplane ever built. (Gloster Photo).

Supermarine S-5. A pair of these captured 1st and 2nd in the 1927 Schneider Trophy race. (Supermarine Photo).

Lt. Al Williams' Curtiss-Kirkham racer was built for the 1927 Schneider but was not ready in time. (Packard Mtr. Co. Photo).

Short "Crusader," also intended for the '27 Schneider, but this British racer crashed during pre-race trials. (Short Bros. Photo).

Italian Macchi M-52 dropped out during 2nl lap of 1927 Schneider race. (Macchi Photo).

Art Goebel and Lt. Bill Davis won the Dole San Francisco-Honolulu race in this modified Travel Air "6000." (Beech Photo).

a 31.07-mile course. Entries were two new Curtiss R3C-1's powered with a new Curtiss V-12 of 620 hp, and flown by Navy Lt. Al Williams and Army Lt. Cy Bettis; two Navy PW-8's piloted by Lts. Cuddihy and Norton; an Army PW-8 flown by Capt. Cook, plus a standard Army pursuit, P-1, with Lt. Dawson at the controls.

The planes took off at ten-second intervals and, although all shared the course simultaneously, each was separately timed. Bettis and Williams set up a nice groove at about 300 feet, with the rest trailing at slightly higher and lower altitudes. Bettis' craft seemed a bit better tuned, and he gradually pulled away from Williams to win with a speed of 249 mph. Williams' average was 241.7 mph. Cuddihy was forced down with engine trouble, and Lt. Dawson took third in the P-1 averaging 169.9 mph. Morton was close behind with 168.8 mph.

This was the last Pulitzer Trophy race. It also marked the end of Army pursuit-plane development for a number of years because the Army—then in the hands of infantry and cavalry generals—decreed that no more money would be spent on racing planes. They sealed this order with the court martial of Billy Mitchell a couple of months later—on December 17, (ironically, the anniversary of the Wright Brothers' first flight) 1925.

Mitchell was "busted" for sassing his superiors (superiors in *rank,* that is), and for trying to awaken the United States to its need for a strong Air Force. (An interesting sidelight to the Mitchell trial is that one of the men who sat in judgment of him was General Douglas MacArthur. After the verdict was read and the courtroom vacated, an enterprising reporter retrieved the judges' ballots from a wastebasket. According to that reporter, Douglas MacArthur was the only one on the court martial board to vote for acquittal).

THE SCHNEIDER TROPHY RACE of 1925 saw the United States as host nation because of Navy Lt. Rittenhouse's victory in 1923 (the Schneider had not been held in 1924). This year it was held at Bay Shore Park, Md., near Baltimore, on October 26. And the pre-race trials were almost as interesting as the race itself. First, England's Supermarine S-4 stalled and dropped 50 feet into the water. Then, England's Gloster III came down hard in rough water and its whole undercarriage collapsed. The Brit-

44

C. W. Parkhurst and R. C. Lowes, Jr. decided not to start in '27 Dole race because of "Air King's" limited fuel supply. (Photo: Steve Hudek).

Spokane Spokesman-Review Trophy of 1927 saw this Curtiss XP-6, flown by Lt. Lyon, in second place at 189.6 mph. (Photo: U.S.A.F.).

Lt. Tom Jeter flew Boeing F4B-1 (without bomb) to win 1928 Pulitzer race. (Boeing Photo).

F/O Waghorn of the R.A.F. won 1929 Schneider race in this Supermarine S-6 with an average speed of 328.6 mph. (Supermarine Photo).

Gloster VI "Golden Arrow" dropped out of '29 Schneider after averaging 336.3 mph. (Gloster Photo).

Al Williams' "Mercury" was built for '29 Schneider but did not participate. (Photo: Jack McRae).

ish had one entry left for the contest, a second Gloster III. It was powered with a Napier Lion 12 cylinder W-type engine of 700 hp. This craft was flown by Capt. Broad.

The Italian entry was a Macchi M-33, powered with a 435-hp Curtiss D-12 engine and flown by Giovanni de Briganti.

For the United States, the Army R3C-1 was fitted with floats and piloted by Lt. Jimmy Doolittle (this was the same plane flown by Lt. Cy Bettis in the Pulitzer earlier in the month). The U.S. Navy entered its R3C-1, plus another identical ship completed since the Pulitzer. The Navy pilots were Lts. George Cuddihy and Ralph Ofstie.

The racecourse was a triangle, 31.07 miles around, with 7 laps required—a total of 217.5 miles.

It was commonly held that Jimmy Doolittle recognized only two throttle positions in a racing plane: "off," or "wide open." He demanded a lot of an airplane; but he contributed his share, too. And after the other two R3C-1's (on floats they were called R3C-2) were forced down, Doolittle went on to win easily with an average speed of 232.6 mph—a new world's record for seaplanes. He also established new records for 100 and 200 kilometers at 234 mph. Capt. Broad, in the Gloster III, was second at 199.2 mph, and Briganti came in third with an average of 168.4 mph.

Later, Doolittle again raised the world seaplane record when he made four passes over a 3-kilometer straightaway at an average speed of 245.7 mph.

THE 1926 NATIONAL AIR RACES drew more participants than ever. Over 200 airplanes were entered in 19 events which were spread between September 4 and 13. The site was Model Farms Field at Philadelphia. There was a special race for the still-plentiful Curtiss "Jennies;" another for National Guard pilots—which was won in a Jenny—and a race for Army observation planes, won by Capt. Ira Eaker in a Curtiss O-1 Falcon.

On Friday, September 10, the fifth annual MITCHELL TROPHY RACE was flown. All entries in the Mitchell race were Curtiss P-1 Hawks. Nine planes competed, and there was but 3-mph difference between first and ninth place. Lt. L. G. Elliott was the winner with a speed of 160.4 mph.

Savoia-Marchetti S-65, a push-pull type a la Cessna Skymaster meant for '29 Schneider, but didn't race. (Savoia-Marchetti Photo).

Phoebe Omlie and her Monocoupe; runner-up in '29 women's closed-course event at National Air Races. (Mono Aircraft Photo).

Travel Air Model R "Mystery," winner of the first Thompson-sponsored race at 1929 NAR. Pilot, Doug Davis. (Beech Photo).

THE KANSAS CITY ROTARY CLUB TROPHY RACE took the place of the discontinued Pulitzer contest. This event was for a total of 120 miles, and was open to Army and Navy pursuit planes. It attracted 12 entries: 8 Army; 3 Navy; and a lone Marine, (which was, someone observed, approximately the proper ratio when a job was to be done). Lt. George Cuddihy, flying a Navy Boeing FB-3, powered with a 600-hp Packard engine, won first place with 180.5 mph. Army Lt. I. G. Elliott was second at 178.6 mph in a P-2 Hawk. The Marine, Lt. Sandy Sanderson, nursing a faulty engine, wound up seventh.

THE 1926 SCHNEIDER TROPHY RACE took place at Hampton Roads, Va., on November 13. The racecourse was seven laps around a 31.07-mile triangle for a total of 217.5 miles. (The reason for these odd figures is that 31.07 miles is equal to 50 kilometers; 217.5 miles, 350 kilometers. Official air speed records must be recorded in terms of kilometers by international agreement).

Two countries, Italy and the United States, each entered three aircraft. The Italian planes were identical Macchi M-39's, powered with 800-hp Fiat V-12 engines. They were flown by Maj. Mario D. Bernardi, Capt. Arturo Farrarini and Lt. Adriano Bacula, all of the Royal Italian Air Force.

United States' entries were the Navy's pair of R3C Curtiss racers, the R3C Army Curtiss, in which Doolittle had won the previous year's Schneider and which was now on loan to the Navy for this contest, plus a Navy Curtiss F6C-1 Hawk held in reserve. U.S. team pilots were Lts. Cuddihy and W. G. Tomlinson of the Navy and Lt. C. F. Schilt of the Marines. Tomlinson cracked up one of the R3C's during pre-race trials, but qualified the F6C-1 Hawk, though it was obviously too slow to stand much of a chance.

The race was well flown by all participants though marred by two drop-outs. One of these was particularly painful because Lt. Cuddihy had second place cinched when his fuel pump failed within sight of the finish line. Maj. de Bernardi placed first with 246.5 mph; Lt. Schilt was second with an average of 231.4 mph, and Lt. Bacula of the Italian team third at 218 mph. The best Lt. Tomlinson could do in the Hawk was 137 mph, but this was good enough for fourth place after Capt. Farrarini was forced out with engine trouble.

Curtiss XP-3A racer, second in 1929 Thompson race. (U.S.A.F. Photo).

Lockheed Air Express, flown to victory by Henry Brown in 1929 Los Angeles to Cleveland race. (General Tire Photo).

"Carr Special," made from parts of a Travel Air biplane; a pure "grass-roots racing effort. (Photo: Steve Hudek).

THE DOLE RACE, SAN FRANCISCO TO HONOLULU, was sponsored by J. D. Dole, president of the Hawaiian Pineapple Company. He offered $35,000 (25 grand for first place, 10 for second) to the winners. Race day was August 16, 1927, and the eight starters were: Martin Jensen and Paul Schluter in a Breese monoplane, the "Aloha;" Art Goebel and Navy Lt. Bill Davis in a Travel Air monoplane, "Woolaroc;" Augie Pedlar and Mildred Doran flying a Buhl Air Sedan, "Miss Doran;" Jack Frost, Pinky Knope and Gordon Scott in the San Francisco *Examiner's* "Golden Eagle;" Bennett Griffin in the "Oklahoma;" Norm Goddard flying "El Encanto;" Livingston Irving in "Pabco Pacific Flier" and Capt. Bill Erwin piloting "Dallas Spirit.'"

Irving and Goddard each crashed on take off. Erwin and Griffin returned to San Francisco with mechanical trouble. "Miss Doran", containing Pedlar and the beautiful Mildred Doran, was lost at sea, as was the "Golden Eagle" and its three crew members. Of the two planes that made it to Hawaii, Art Goebel's Travel Air was first, with a time of 26 hours and 17 minutes. Martin Jensen, in "Aloha," landed one hour and 58 minutes later.

THE NATIONAL AIR RACES of 1927, at Spokane, Washington, September 19-25, were attended by more cowboys and Indians than any air races before or since. There were a lot of other people there, too. And there was plenty for them to see: a wild free-for-all for civilian planes, daily exhibitions in aerobatics and military precision formation flying; a special race between Army observation craft—won by Lt. Johnson in a Curtiss Falcon at 170 mph — and several "On to Spokane" races originating in other parts of the nation. Charles "Speed" Holman won the New York Spokane Class A race in a Laird Speedwing.

THE SPOKANE SPOKESMAN-REVIEW TROPHY, offered to the winner of a free-for-all for military pursuits, was the main event of the Spokane meet. Six Army and four Navy planes entered, with Army Lt. Batten, in an XP-6 Hawk, taking first place. His average speed was 201.2-mph. Lt. Lyon, also flying an Army XP-6 Curtiss Hawk, was second, followed by three Navy FB-5 Boeings.

THE SCHNEIDER TROPHY RACE of 1927 was flown from Venice, Italy's Lido Beach, on September 26. England and Italy each

Gee Bee Sportster flown by Lowell Bayles in 1930 Cirrus cross-country race. (Photo: Steve Hudek).

Great Lakes 2T1, one of five of this kind entered in 1930 Cirrus race.

Cirrus race entry R-12E. This one stumped us. (Photo: Steve Hudek).

Cessna GC-1, Cirrus race entry flown by Stan Stanton. (Photo: Steve Hudek).

Laird Solution, winner of 1930 Thompson. Billy Brock in cockpit. (Photo: Steve Hudek).

Curtiss XF6C-6, special Navy racer in which Marine Capt. Page met his death during 1930 Thompson Trophy Race. (Navy Photo).

Cessna GC-2 racer, powered with 110 hp Warner, and built for 1930 races. (U.S.A.F. Photo).

Jim Haizlip and his Travel Air Model R "Mystery" in which he won 2nd place in 1930 Thompson race. (Shell Oil Co. Photo).

Travel Air "3000," fitted with Wright J-6 engine, was flown to 4th place in '30 Thompson by Paul Adams. (Beech Photo).

qualified three planes. The single U.S. entry, Al Williams' Packard-Kirkham biplane, was not completed in time. The English planes were 2 Supermarine S-5's aand a Gloster IV, all powered with the Napier Lion W-type engine of 875-hp.

The wings of the S-5's were covered with smooth brass radiators and the fuselage-sides constituted the oil-cooling radiators. Fuel was carried in the right-hand float to counteract torque. England also readied a new radial-engine Short Crusader—possibly as a replacement for one of the S-5's—but aileron controls were accidently crossed during assembly and it crashed on a test flight.

Italy's hopes for the race were represented in three identical Macchi M-52's, powered with V-12 Fiat engines of 1030-hp.

The contest consisted of the usual 7 laps around a 31.07-mile course, although the triangle was laid out in such a manner that two of the turns were almost 180 degrees. Despite this penalty, it was immediately clear that new speeds would be reached; Lt. Kinkead's Gloster IV turned the first lap at 277 mph—an all-time speed record for biplanes.

Kinkhead was forced down after three laps, however, with a broken prop shaft. Flt. Lt. Webster, flying an S-5, took the lead and remained there. One by one the Italian planes dropped out (all of them were later found to have defective pistons), and the race ended with Webster in first place, averaging 281.7 mph and Flt. Lt. Worsley bringing in the second S-5 at 273.1 mph.

THE NATIONAL AIR RACES OF 1928 were held at Mines Field, Los Angeles, September 8-16, and drew more than a quarter-million spectators. There were three transcontinental races from Roosevelt Field, N. Y., and the fastest of these was won by Bob Cantwell, flying a new Lockheed Vega. His elapsed time was 24 hours and 9 minutes.

THE MITCHELL TROPHY RACE, with 10 Curtiss P-1A's competing, was won by Lt. E. H. Lawson at 154.7 mph.

Event #12, open to all military planes, drew only Navy entrants. A new Boeing XF4B pursuit, flown by Lt. Jeter, easily took this one over five older F2B's. The winning speed over the 6-lap 60-mile course was 172.3 mph.

The Detroit *News* sponsored an unlimited free-for-all for

Ben Howard's "Pete," with a Wright "Gipsy" engine, placed third in 1930 Thompson race. (Photo: Steve Hudek).

Frank Hawks and his J-6-powered Travel Air dropped out of 1930 Thompson. Two weeks before, however, he had set a Los Angeles-New York record with speed of 215 mph. (Photo: The Texas Co.).

Jimmy Doolittle and his Laird "Super Solution"; winner of 1931 Bendix; dropped out of Thompson in 7th lap. (Photo: Steve Hudek).

civilian aircraft, and Bob Cantwell's Wasp-powered Vega barely beat out Art Goebel's Vega to take this one. Average speeds were 140.3 mph and 139.7 mph respectively. Roscoe Turner, flying his first race, was last in a field of eight.

There was no SCHNEIDER TROPHY RACE in 1928, it having been decided to hold this contest every other year.

THE NATIONAL AIR RACES OF 1929 were the biggest ever, and marked the beginning of a new era in racing — the emergence of civilian airplanes that were far superior to the best that the impoverished military services could offer. The Nationals were held at Cleveland, August 24 to September 2, and more than half a million paid to see the show.

There were several "On to Cleveland" races and a total of 27 closed-course events. Many outstanding aerobatic pilots performed, among them Jimmy Doolittle. And when Jimmy's Curtiss P-1 shed its wings while he was wringing it out a couple of miles from the race area, Jimmy took to his "rag bag," then hurried back for another plane and continued his exhibition. There were giants in those days.

A woman's race, from Santa Monica to Cleveland, was won by Louise Thaden in her Travel Air biplane, with a total flying time of 20 hours, 2 minutes. Gladys O'Donnell was second and Amelia Earhart third.

A special non-stop race from Los Angeles had but two entries. However, the winner, Henry Brown in a Lockheed Air Express, furnished an exciting finish when he ran out of gas in the final approach to his landing. He coasted dead-stick across the finish line. His average speed was 186 mph (13 hours, 15 minutes). Lee Shoenhair landed 36 minutes later flying a Lockheed Vega.

In THE MITCHELL TROPHY RACE, Lt. Wurtsmith, in a P-1B Hawk, circled the 12-lap 10-mile course at an average of 152.2 mph to take first place.

A race limited to civilian cabin-types was taken by Bob Cantwell in his Vega with an average of 152.3 mph.

The multi-engine race was won by Waldo Waterman in a 10-place Bach Air Yacht at 136.4 mph. A Wasp-powered tri-motored Fokker F-10 could manage but 123 mph in this contest.

Wiley Post and Winnie Mae. Wiley was winner of 1930 cross-country race in his famous around-the-world plane. (Photo: Steve Hudek).

Gee Bee Model Z and pilot Lowell Bayles, winner of 1931 Thompson Trophy Race. (Thompson Products Photo).

Lowell Bayles, shortly before his death in Gee Bee Model Z. (Photo: Steve Hudek).

Ira Eaker's Lockheed Altair. (U.S.A.F. Photo).

Gee Bee Model Y flown by Maude Tait in 1931 Aerol Trophy race. (Photo: U.S.A.F.).

Jimmy Wedell in his famed Wedell-Williams "Miss Patterson." (U.S.A.F. Photo).

Gladys O'Donnell flew her taperwing Waco to first place in the women's closed-course event. Her speed was 137.6 mph.

The main event was a 5-lap 50-mile unlimited free-for-all sponsored by the Thompson Products Company. Entries were an Army P3A Hawk piloted by Lt. Breene, a Navy Hawk flown by Cmdr. J. J. Clark, Roscoe Turner in his Vega; Conaughey in a Travel Air biplane, and Doug Davis in a new Travel Air Model R, which had been dubbed "Mystery Ship" by reporters because it had been built in secrecy and kept under wraps until race time.

(The Travel Air Company had been founded in 1924 by Walter Beech, Clyde Cessna, and Lloyd Stearman with the help of a few Wichita, Kan. businessmen. By 1929, however, both Stearman and Cessna had pulled out to form companies of their own, leaving Walter Beech in control of Travel Air. Walter sold out to Curtiss-Wright just days before the bottom fell out of the stock market in the fall of 1929. He and his wife Olive Ann started Beech Aircraft Corporation in 1932).

Event #26, as this first Thompson-sponsored race was called, was won by Doug Davis in the Travel Air Mystery. Davis led the second-place P3A Army Hawk by more than eight miles at the finish, and averaged 194.9 mph despite turning around in mid-course to re-circle a pylon he thought he had missed. Roscoe Turner was third, and Cmdr. Clark fourth.

Another noteworthy plane at the 1929 nationals was the Baby Bullet built by Ed Heath — the world's first homebuilt midget racer. In one event the Baby Bullet turned in an average speed of 109.5 mph with its tiny 2-cylinder engine.

THE SCHNEIDER TROPHY RACE OF 1929, at Calshot, England, was flown on September 7. The 7-lap 217.5-mile course was marked by buoys in the water between the Isle of Wight and the Isle of Solent. England entered three planes; Italy three. The U. S. entry, Al Williams' Mercury, had been built by private donations and depended upon Navy sponsorship to get to England; but the Navy backed out and Williams again stayed home.

The Italian effort this year was magnificent; despite loss of her fastest planes and several of her best racing pilots during pre-race tests, Italy nevertheless got three planes together to compete with the British. The Italians held almost no hope of winning, but their spirit would take first place in any man's race.

Bob Hall and his Springfield-Hall "Bulldog," a 1932 Thompson entry. (Photo: U.S.A.F.).

Russ Boardman prepares to test new Gee Bee R-1. Rudder and fin were later enlarged to improve stability. Boardman was fatally injured in this plane in 1933. (Steve Hudek Photo).

Gee Bee R-1 with Jimmy Doolittle at controls won 1932 Thompson race and established landplane speed record. (Shell Oil Co. Photo).

Gee Bee R-2, sister ship to R-1, 1932 Bendix entry. (Tom Granville Photo).

Steve Wittman's "Chief Oshkosh," at 1932 National Air Races. (Steve Hudek Photo).

Jim Haizlip's Wedell-Williams racer; 4th in 1932 Thompson, and after that a perennial prize-winner. (U.S.A.F. Photo).

The Italian racers were a pair of Macchi M-67's and a Macchi M-52. Pilots Monti and Cadringher piloted the 67's; Dal Molin the M-52.

The British entries were two Supermarine S-6's, flown by Waghorn and Atcherly, and an older S-5 with Flt. Off. Greig at its controls. The S-6 was slightly heavier and more powerful than the S-5.

The racers were flagged into the air shortly after lunch, and Flt. Lt. Waghorn, in an S-6, took the lead at once. Monti was forced down with a broken oil line during the first lap; Cadringher, in the second M-67, then faltered onto the water almost overcome by engine fumes. This left only the old M-52 for Italy. However, Atcherly, in one of the S-6's, missed a pylon and was disqualified. This cut the field to Waghorn who, in the other S-6, clearly had the race won, and the two old "back up" planes. Waghorn's winning speed was 328.6 mph, and the Italian Dal Molin barely squeezed by Greig to take second with a speed of 284.2 mph.

THE ALL AMERICAN FLYING DERBY (CIRRUS RACE), of 1930, was flown over a course 5,541 miles long! On July 21, eighteen civilian planes took off from Detroit, flew south to Texas, west to California, then back to Detroit. Ten planes finished the race with Lee Gehlbach taking first at 127.11 mph and Lowell Bayles second at 116.4 mph. Gehlbach's plane was a Commandaire Rocket. Bayles flew a Gee Bee Sportster — the first in a line of famous racing planes. Other participants were: H. H. Ogden in an Ogden Osprey; five Great Lakes biplanes piloted by C. W. Meyers, W. H. Cahill, W. H. Holliday, Joe Meehan and Cecil Coffrin; a Cessna CR-1 racer with Stanley Stanton at its controls; Jimmy Wedell in a Wedell-Williams Special — another prototype of some famous racers to come; Russ Hosler in a G & G Special; J. Kruttschmitt flying an English DeHavilland Moth; Mummert Mercury flown by Harvey Mummert; E. B. Todd in an Alexander Special; B.B. Smith piloting a Pacific School of Engineering Special; Stan Quimby in a Mono Sport; Herman Hamer flying a Laird and Larry Brown driving the California Cub. Seven of these planes were stock models. The rest were either "modified stocks" (eleven were supercharged) or had been built especially for this race. All wore Cirrus engines.

Ben Howard's "Ike," often in the win-column of the 500 cu. in. races, made its appearance in 1932. (Steve Hudek Photo).

Cessna CR-1 (later, CR-2 and CR-2A) "Miss Wanda," was flown by Roy Liggett. Broke-up in air at Chicago races. (Cessna Photo).

Gordon Israel's "Redhead" first raced at Cleveland, 1932. (Steve Hudek Photo).

which was a necessary qualification set down by the sponsor, American Cirrus Engine Company of Marysville, Michigan.

THE 1930 NATIONAL AIR RACES were held at Chicago's Curtiss-Reynolds Airport, August 23 to September 1. In addition to the three dozen closed-course events, six cross-country races were featured. Wiley Post won the Los Angeles-Chicago Race in his famous Lockheed Vega, Winnie Mae. His competition consisted of three other Vegas and a Lockheed Air Express. Of three military races, the fastest time was turned in by Marine Lt. Sandy Sanderson, flying a Wasp-powered Curtiss Sea Hawk. Sandy, it will be remembered, had been a regular contender at the air races since the Pulitzer days. A great gentleman and a fine flier, it must have saddened him to see a Ford trimotor airliner, during a later race, equal the speed of the best pursuit plane the Navy possessed—142 mph. The Navy was just as guilty as the Army in neglecting development of the airplane between WW I and WW II.

A crowd favorite was Ben O. Howard and his saucy little homebuilt racer, Pete. Pete had but 90 hp but it took first place in five closed-course events, each time competing against planes of higher horsepower. In one contest, Howard averaged 163 mph.

Gladys O'Donnell won the Women's Class A Pacific Derby by flying from Long Beach to Chicago in 15 hours, 13 minutes, in her taperwing Waco. Gladys also took charge of the money in the Women's Free-For-All with a speed of 149.9 mph.

THE THOMPSON TROPHY RACE OF 1930 was the first of a series of 10 — 1930 through 1939 inclusive — which was to provide the greatest spectacle that air racing has ever seen. Due to the popularity and success of the 50-mile free-for-all that Thompson Products Company had sponsored at the 1929 nationals, the Thompson Trophy — to be kept in possession of the winner and passed on each year — was offered in addition to a $5,000 cash prize. The racecourse was a five-mile triangle, and the race was for 20 laps.

There were seven entries: Jim Haizlip in a Travel Air Mystery; Frank Hawks, also in a Travel Air Mystery (and in which he had just crossed the U.S. from Los Angeles to New York in 12 hours, 25 minutes — an average of 215 mph including gas stops); Paul Adams, flying a Travel Air Speedwing biplane;

Laird Solution powered with a Menasco engine, was an entry in the 500 cu. in. races. (Steve Hudek Photo).

John Livingston and his Cessna CR-3 racer competed at Omaha, Minneapolis, Chicago and Cleveland. This was fastest of all Cessna racers, (1933). (Steve Hudek Photo).

Heath-Owens "Cannonball," a 500 cu. in. hopeful. (Photo: Steve Hudek).

Macchi-Castoldi MC-72 had two Isotta-Fraschini engines set in tandem and contra-rotating props. It established world speed record of 440.7 mph on June 2, 1933. (Macchi Photo).

Gee Bee Q.E.D., built for London-Melbourne race, also entered in 1934 Bendix.

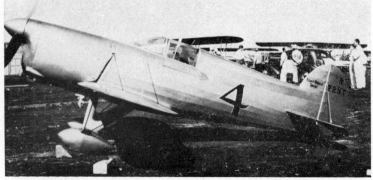

Lee Miles' Miles & Atwood Special began its career at the 1934 National Air Races. (Steve Hudek Photo).

Erett Williams in a Wedell-Williams (Erett was scheduled to fly a Cessna CR-1 racer but switched at the last minute); Ben Howard lined up in his formidable homebuilt, Pete; Marine Capt. Arthur Page in the only military entry, the Curtiss XF6C-6, a greatly-modified Hawk; and a Laird Solution, flown by Speed Holman, which had just rolled out of Matty Laird's Chicago factory a half hour before the race.

The Thompson's famous "race horse starts" were not begun until the following year, and in this race the contestants were flagged into the air at 10-second intervals. Capt. Page was away first, followed by Howard, Haizlip, Williams, Holman and Adams. Page continued to lead until the 17th lap when his plane went out of control and crashed. It was later determined that he had been overcome by carbon monoxide fumes. He died the next day.

Frank Hawks had dropped out in the third lap with engine trouble, and Williams was forced down in the 8th lap. Holman crept up on Haizlip, passed him, and was leading at the finish. Holman's speed was 201.9 mph; Haizlip's 199.8 mph. Ben Howard was third in Pete — a plane with less than one-fourth the horsepower of the first and second-place winners. Paul Adams was fourth.

THE 1931 NATIONAL AIR RACES were at Cleveland, August 29, to September 7. Purses were increased and so was the competition. The new Bendix Trophy gathered the various cross-country races into a single, grand free-for-all; it was open to both men and women and to any kind of plane. There were 28 closed-course events, capped by the Big One — the Thompson.

THE BENDIX TROPHY RACE was flown from Burbank, California, to Cleveland. The participants were Jimmy Doolittle in a Laird Super Solution; Harold Johnson (a man noted for his ability to loop a 6-ton Ford Trimotor from ground-level), and Beeler Blevins, each in a Lockheed Orion, and Ira Eaker in a Lockheed Altair. They arrived in Cleveland in that order — Jimmy with an average of 223.03 mph (including fuel stops). Doolittle then proceeded to New York for a new transcontinental record of 11 hours, 16 minutes, 10 seconds elapsed time for the 2,450-mile distance. And an hour later he was back in Cleveland to claim his loot.

Roy Minor (L) with Al Menasco and the Brown Special, "Miss Los Angeles." (Steve Hudek Photo).

Roscoe Turner and his Hornet-powered Wedell-Williams. (U.S.A.F. Photo).

Howard "Mike," brother to "Ike" and "Pete," at the 1934 Nationals. (Steve Hudek Photo).

Art Chester's Menasco-powered "Jeep." (Steve Hudek Photo).

"Mike" stubs toe during 500 cu. in. race. (Steve Hudek Photo).

English pilots Scott and Black flew this DH "Comet" to first place in the London-Melbourne race of 1934. (Flight Photo).

THE THOMPSON TROPHY RACE was a 10-lap 100-miler this year, with eight planes entered. Lined up for the first "race horse start" were: Doolittle in his green-and-white Super Solution; Lowell Bayles in the sensational new Gee Bee Model Z, "City of Springfield"; Dale Jackson, flying the Laird Solution that Holman had won with the year before; Jimmy Wedell in his Wedell Williams Special; Bob Hall in a Gee Bee Model Y; Ira Eaker at the controls of his Lockheed Altair; Bill Ong piloting a Laird Speedwing and Ben Howard in Pete.

The green flag dropped and it was every man for himself. The planes first headed for a scattering pylon placed a mile off the course, then roared back to actually begin the race — although they were timed from the sweep of the starter's flag. Doolittle was first around the scattering pylon with Bayles right behind. In the second lap, Bayles took the lead when Jimmy's plane scuffed a piston and began pouring smoke. Dale Jackson, running third, struck a tree but kept going.

Doolittle held on to second position until the seventh lap when his engine at last quit altogether. Bayles was never seriously threatened by any of the others; he took the checkered flag well out in front with an average of 236.2 mph. Wedell was second and Jackson third. Hall, in the Gee Bee Model Y, nosed out Eaker for fourth place.

The Gee Bee Model Y ("Senior Sportster") was actually a two-placer with its front cockpit covered over for racing. On the day before the Thompson was flown, Maude Tait flew it to first place in the Aerol Trophy Race for women at an average speed of 187.6 mph — a closed course record for girl-type fliers. It was powered with a 420-hp Pratt & Whitney Wasp.

The Gee Bee Model Z, "City of Springfild," was a smaller plane than the Y Model, but was powered with a souped-up 535-hp Wasp. It was, of course, a pure racer. It won every event in which it was entered, including, in addition to the Thompson, the 50-mile Goodyear Trophy Race, the General Tire & Rubber Trophy, and a mixed free-for-all.

On December 5, 1931, Bayles died in the Model Z when it shed a wing during an attempt to establish a new landplane speed record. The Model Z's true top speed was never clearly determined, although Bayles was clocked at 314 mph on one pass

Boeing 247D airliner carried Roscoe Turner and Clyde Pangborn to 3rd place in London-Melbourne race. (Rudy Arnold Photo).

Bellanca "Flash" was designed as a long-distance racer. Jim Mollison flew this plane from Newfoundland to London in 13 hours, 17 minutes. (Photo: Leo Kohn).

Ben Howard's "Mr. Mulligan" took both Bendix and Thompson in 1935—while "Mike" won the '35 Greve Trophy. (Steve Hudek Photo).

over the official course before the plane was lost. At that time, the world's landplane speed record, held by France, was 278.48 mph.

THE SCHNEIDER TROPHY RACE OF 1931, again held at Lee-on-Solent, England, wasn't really a race but it did gain for Britain permanent possession of this trophy. It took place on September 13. The English had two new Supermarine S-6B's ready — principally because Lady Houston had donated almost half a-million dollars for their construction and testing — and was not to be denied the fruits of such preparation, even though there was no competition.

France backed-out at the last minute, and Italy was forced out because of the loss of several racers and pilots. The United States, of course, had no entry. Participation in the Schneider demanded far more capital outlay than an individual could muster; and the U.S. Army and Navy were spending their money on saddle horses and battleships, not airplanes.

With thousands watching from the shore, and Lady Houston viewing proceedings from her private yacht, Flt. Lt. J. H. Boothman thundered around the 31.07-mile course seven times at an average speed of 340.1 mph. A few minutes later, Lt. Stainforth assaulted the world's speed record in the second S-6B. He lanced over the 3-kilometer course six times for an average of 379.1 mph to gain the record for England.

Still not satisfied, the British installed a new Rolls Royce V-12 engine in Lt. Stainforth's S-6B and, on September 29, he made the minimum required four passes over the course, this time averaging 407 mph. This was the engine that later became the famous Merlin of WW II — and the Supermarine S-6B was the natural father of the Spitfire. Clearly, Lady Houston's money was well spent.

THE NATIONAL AIR RACES OF 1932 were at Cleveland, August 27 to September 5. Ben Howard was back with two new racers, Ike and Mike, to "share the wealth" with Pete. Between them they took 3 firsts and 3 seconds in the limited-horsepower contests. Ben himself, however, had to be content to remain on the ground; the airline that employed him had forbidden him to race.

73

Lockheed Orion flown by Roy Hunt in '35 Bendix. (Photo: Joe Barry).

Northrup 2E "Gamma," was entered in '35 Bendix by Bernarr Mac-Fadden, but cracked-up prior to the race. (Steve Hudek).

Ross Hadley's Staggerwing Beech (D17S) placed fifth in the 1938 Bendix. (Leo Kohn Photo).

74

Seversky SEV-3L, converted to amphibian, was flown in the 1935 Thompson by Lee Miles. (Seversky Photo).

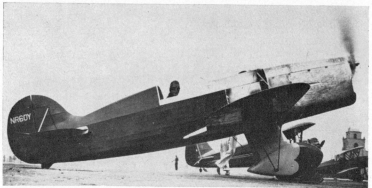

Dave Elmendorf in his Menasco-powered Wedell-Williams, a 1935 Greve Trophy entry. (Steve Hudek Photo).

Howard Hughes established new landplane speed record in this specially-built racer in 1935. (Steve Hudek Photo).

Steve Wittman's new Cirrus-powered Chief Oshkosh also won a limited race. And the Granville Brothers' Gee Bees had another banner year. Previously, a Gee Bee Sportster Model E, flown by C. A. Nott, had won the Cuban Trophy at Miami, Fla. Then, Russ Boardman claimed the feature event at the Omaha Air Races in a Gee Bee Model Y. He repeated this performance at the Niagara Falls International Air Races in the same plane.

At Cleveland, two new Gee Bees appeared. Outwardly they were twins, although the R-1, #11, had an 800-hp Wasp Senior engine to make it go, while the R-2, #7, featured a big gas tank and 535 hp to better suit it for the Bendix.

THE 1932 BENDIX was flown from Burbank to Cleveland on August 29. Entries were three Wedell-Williams Specials, piloted by Jim Haizlip, Jimmy Wedell and Roscoe Turner, and the Gee Bee R-2, #7, with Lee Gehlbach at the stick. They finished in that order. Haizlip's time was 8 hours, 19 minutes, 45 seconds. The Gee Bee R-2 was plagued with engine trouble all the way and, though many believed it to be the fastest plane entered, its arrival in Cleveland was 1 hour and 20 minutes behind the lead plane. Haizlip continued to New York and clipped 57 minutes from Doolittle's record of the year before. He had averaged 245 mph to Cleveland, and 238.2 for the coast-to-coast record.

THE 1932 AEROL TROPHY RACE FOR WOMEN dispelled notions that the girls were strictly fair-weather pilots. A thunderstorm broke during the second lap and, although race officials tried to flag them down, only Gladys O'Donnell and Mae Haizlip (Jimmy's wife) saw the flags and landed after 5 laps. Betty Lund (wife of famed stunt flier Fred Lund) and Florence Klingensmith completed the full 8 laps although they were merely guessing as to where the pylons were located. First place was awarded to Gladys, flying Ben Howard's Mike, on the basis of the standings at the 5-lap mark. Her average was 185.5 mph. Florence piloted Johnny Livingston's clipped-wing Monocoupe, Betty was in an open-cockpit Waco, and Mae Haizlip was flying her husband's Wedell-Williams Special.

In the Gee Bee R-1's first appearance, Jimmy Doolittle blasted over the 3-kilometer Shell Qualifying Course 4 times at an average speed of 294.4 mph to establish a new landplane speed

Harold Neumann's Folkerts "Toots," fourth in '36 Thompson. (Aero Digest Photo).

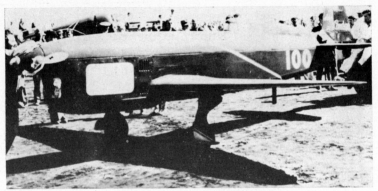

Michel Detroyat of France piloted this Caudron racer to first place in both Thompson and Greve races of 1936. (Steve Hudek Photo).

Harry Crosby and his homebuilt Thompson Trophy racer, (Steve Hudek Photo).

Earl Ortman and his Keith-Rider; 2nd in 1936 Thompson. (Steve Hudek Photo).

Louise Thaden flew her blue-and-white Staggerwing Beech (C17R-81) to first place in the 1936 Bendix race. (Beech Photo).

Laura Ingalls was second in '36 Bendix flying this Lockheed Orion. Here she talks with Wiley Post (R) and Billy Parker. (Billy Parker Photo).

record. The old record, held by France, had been set in 1924 by Lt. Bonnett in a Ferbois monoplane.

THE 1932 THOMPSON TROPHY RACE, 10 laps around a 10-mile course, was flown on Monday afternoon, September 5. The "Big Daddy" of closed-course air racing events again drew eight contestants: Jimmy Doolittle in the Gee Bee R-1; Lee Gehlbach flying the Gee Bee R-2; Wedell, Turner and Haizlip in their Wedell-Williams Specials; Bob Hall, a former employee of Granville Brothers and co-designer of past Gee Bees, piloting a new gull-wing racer of his own design; Bill Ong in Howard's Ike and Ray Moore in a new Keith Rider Special, "San Francisco I."

With the quick chop of the green flag and the boom of a mortar the racers were off in a race-horse start. Hall was first around the scattering pylon, but Doolittle passed him almost at once and began pulling away. In the second lap, Ray Moore dropped out with engine trouble and Hall fell back into sixth place. Jimmy Wedell moved up to second place, Turner third, Haizlip fourth, Gehlbach fifth and Ong brought up the rear. The race ended in that order. Jimmy Doolittle lapped the entire field at least once and roared over the finish line trailing smoke and pulling farther ahead with each revolution of the Gee Bee's 8-ft. prop. His average speed, a new closed-course record, was 252.7 mph. Wedell, in second place, had 242.5 mph.

THE 1933 NATIONAL AIR RACES were held at Los Angeles, July 1-4. In the limited-displacement closed-course events, George Hague, in the Keith Rider Bumblebee, and Roy Minor in Ben Howard's Mike, took more than their share of the prize money. Steve Wittman won the 550-cubic-inch Sweepstakes at 159.8 mph at the controls of Chief Oshkosh.

Steve's little plane, like those of Ben Howard and, indeed, like most of the racers competing at the NAR, should be classed as "homebuilt." Even the Wedell-Williams Specials and the Gee Bees — the fastest landplanes in the world — belonged more to this class than any other. All were produced on the proverbial shoestring; built in the corner of a hangar or in someone's backyard. The Gee Bees had a factory of sorts, an abandoned dance pavilion in Springfield, Mass. And although the Granville Brothers considered themselves commercial aircraft manufac-

Amelia Earhart entered her new Lockheed "Electra" in the '36 Bendix. Amelia was lost (with Navigator Fred Noonan) in this plane. (Steve Hudek Photo).

Ortman's revamped Keith-Rider, known as a Marcoux-Bromberg in 1937, took second in '37 Thompson. (Steve Hudek Photo).

Folkerts Special flown by Roger Don Rae. (Steve Hudek Photo).

turers, their total output from 1929 to 1934 consisted of 9 biplanes, 9 Gee Bee Sportsters (110-125 hp), 2 Model Y Senior Sportsters — not thought of as racers by the Granvilles, though they were used for little else — and 5 pure racers.

THE AEROL TROPHY RACE FOR WOMEN was taken by Mae Haizlip in her husband's Wedell-Williams. Marty Bowman placed second flying a Gee Bee Model Y, followed by Gladys O'Donnell in her taperwing Waco and Helen Sumner in a Travel Air biplane.

THE BENDIX TROPHY RACE was flown from New York to Los Angeles this year, and Roscoe Turner, whose Wedell-Williams Special had been fitted with a 900-hp Hornet, made the flight in 11 hours and 30 minutes for an average speed of 214.8 mph (including 4 refueling stops), thus establishing a new east-west trans-continental record.

None of the other four entries finished. Russell Thaw, flying the Gee Bee R-2, #7, ground-looped at Indianapolis and decided to go no farther. Russ Boardman, in the Gee Bee R-1, #11, lost control and crashed while taking off from the Indianapolis fuel stop. He later died of injuries suffered in the mishap. Lee Gehlbach was forced down with mechanical trouble, and Amelia Earhart dropped out at Wichita with an overheated engine.

THE 1933 THOMPSON TROPHY RACE drew six entries: three Wedell-Williams Specials, flown by Roscoe Turner, Lee Gehlbach and Jim Wedell; Roy Minor in Mike; Zantford "Granny" Granville flying a Gee Bee Model Y and George Hague in the Keith Rider Bumblebee.

The race consisted of 6 laps around the 10-mile course. At the start, Turner took the lead with Wedell close behind. Gehlbach was in third place, Roy Minor fourth. In the second lap Turner missed a pylon, and though he circled back in an attempt to make it up, was disqualified. Wedell moved into first and remained there (Turner actually re-passed Wedell and finished with a higher average speed, but this was not officially recognized). Wedell's first place average was 238 mph. Lee Gehlbach was second with 224.9 mph and Roy Minor flew Mike to third place at 199.9 mph.

Rudy Kling's Folkerts "Jupiter," took first in '37 Thompson Race. (Photo: Warren Bodie Archives).

Matty Laird (L) and Roscoe Turner with the Laird-Turner Special and Roscoe's old Wedell-Williams racer. (Photo: Turner Aeronautical Corp.)

Frank Fuller and his Seversky SEV-S2 (P-35) in which he won the 1937 Bendix Trophy Race. (Seversky Photo).

Jackie Cochran's Staggerwing Beech (D17W). Jackie placed third in the 1937 Bendix. (Beech Photo).

Jackie Cochran's Seversky SEV-S2; first in '38 Bendix. (Jack McRae Photo).

Pearson-Williams "Mr. Smoothie," failed to prove itself at the Nationals. (Steve Hudek Photo).

THE CHICAGO INTERNATIONAL AIR RACES OF 1933 were held September 1-4 as the official aviation event of the Chicago World's Fair. During race preliminaries, Jim Wedell set a new landplane speed record of 305.33 mph in his Wedell-Williams Special.

THE CHICAGO DAILY NEWS TROPHY RACE was for planes in the 550-cubic-inch engine displacement class. Roy Minor won this one in Mike, claiming a new class record of 201.33 mph. Gordon Israel, flying his own creation, Redhead, was second and Art Chester third in the Chester Jeep.

THE FRANK PHILLIPS TROPHY RACE, a hundred-mile unlimited free-for-all, was the main event of the World's Fair air races. Sponsored by the Phillips Petroleum Company, this contest offered a total of $10,000 in prize money.

The race was flown on Labor Day, September 4, and was marked by tragedy. Twenty-six-year-old Florence Klingensmith crashed to her death in the 7th lap when fabric peeled from the right wing of her Gee Bee Model Y. She had flown a marvelous race and was bunched with the leaders when her plane smashed to earth out of control. Jim Wedell went on to win the Phillips. Lee Gehlbach was second and Roy Minor third. Roscoe Turner, Lee Miles, and Steve Wittman dropped out.

Another famous racing pilot to die at Chicago that day was Roy Liggett. Roy was flying his Cessna CR-2, and in a 2,000-ft. dive over the 3-kilometer speed course his plane broke up at an altitude too low to permit him a chance to escape with his parachute.

An event that was spawned by the discontinued Schneider Trophy Races took place in 1934 and may be of interest. On October 23, Italian Francesco Agello flew a Macchi-Castoldi MC-72 seaplane over a regulation 3-kilometer course at Lake Garda to establish a new world's record of 440.68 mph. It was five years before an airplane of any type bettered this mark (a souped-up Messerschmitt Me-109R landplane), and to this day, no seaplane has ever equalled it. The MC-72 had two Fiat V-12 engines set in tandem but operating independently. The drive shaft of the rear engine extended between the V cylinder banks of the forward one, thus delivering a total of 3,000 hp to the contra-rotating props.

Tony LeVier's Schoenfeldt "Firecracker." (Photo: Warren Bodie Archives).

Steve Wittman's "Bonzo," third in 1938 Thompson race.

Bellanca trimotor 28-92, flown to second place in 1939 Bendix by Art Bussy. (Bellanca Photo).

Roscoe Turner took Thompson in 1938 and 1939 with Laird-Turner "Pesco Special" (formerly "Meteor"). (Steve Hudek Photo).

Modified Wedell-Williams with cantilever wing and retractable landing gear did not race. (Steve Hudek Photo).

Military Aircraft Co. HM-1, formerly Hawks' "Time Flies," placed 4th in '38 Thompson with Leigh Wade at controls. (Hudek Photo).

THE 1934 NATIONAL AIR RACES saw the inauguration of an important new contest — the Louis W. Greve Trophy Race. This event was limited to the 550-cubic-inch displacement group, and the winners were determined by a point system: each pilot, flying the same airplane in three races or heats, was credited with 5 points for a 1st place, 4 points for a second, three for a third, etc.

The first Greve Trophy winner was Lee Miles, flying a Miles-Atwood Special powered with a Menasco 225 hp engine. Lee gathered 12 points in the three Greve events, taking a first, a second and a third place. His speeds were 206.2, 203.1 and 203.4 mph. Art Chester in his Jeep, and Roger Don Rae in the Keith Rider San Francisco I, tied for second place with eight points each.

The Nationals were at Cleveland, August 31 to September 3, and although the addition of the Greve events helped to make this one of the biggest meets ever, two of the men who had done the most for air racing were absent. Jimmy Wedell had been killed two months before — while instructing a student in a training plane. And Granny Granville had died in the wreckage of a Gee Bee Sportster on February 12.

THE BENDIX TROPHY RACE opened the 1934 Nationals and was flown from Burbank to Cleveland. Six planes were entered, but only three started. Doug Davis, flying Jimmy Wedell's famed #44, was first with an average of 216.2 mph. J. A. Worthen, in Jim Haizlip's Wedell-Williams, was second with 203.2 mph. A big long-distance two-place Gee Bee, the Q.E.D., designed by the Granvilles before Granny's death and intended for the upcoming London-Melbourne race, was entered by Lee Gehlbach but because of mechanical trouble failed to reach Cleveland ahead of the 6 p.m. deadline.

Roscoe Turner, who entered but did not start in the Bendix, lowered his own coast-to-coast record the next day by flying from Los Angeles to New York at an average speed of 244 mph including fuel stops. And Doug Davis upped the landplane speed record to 306.2 mph with four passes over the Shell qualifying course.

THE THOMPSON TROPHY RACE had six contestants: Roy Minor in the new Brown Special, Miss Los Angeles; Lee Miles flying the

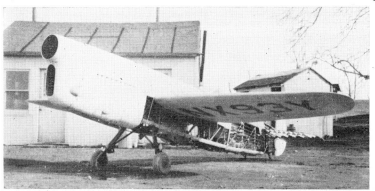

Art Chester's "Goon" under construction. (Leo Kohn Photo).

Gee Bee Q.E.D. after record flight between Mexico City and New York. Pilot: Francisco Sarabia. (Rudy Arnold Photo).

Frank Fuller and Alexander P. deSeversky (R) after Fuller's 1939 Bendix win in Seversky SEV-S2. (Seversky Photo).

Miles and Atwood Special; Art Chester in his Jeep; Roger Don Rae at the throttle of the Keith Rider San Francisco I; Harold Neumann flying Howard's Ike, plus Roscoe Turner, J. Worthen and Doug Davis in a trio of Wedell-Williams Specials. Turner had 1,000 hp in his plane, Doug Davis' #44 could call on a total of 800 horses and Worthen's ship was fitted with a 535-hp Wasp.

At the scattering pylon Doug Davis took the lead and, flying very low and with great precision, gradually increased his advantage until, in the eighth lap, his plane wobbled crazily and plunged into the ground following an unexplained high-speed stall. Davis died instantly. Turner went on to win at 248.1 mph. Roy Minor was second at 214.9 mph.

THE LONDON-TO-MELBOURNE AIR RACE OF 1934 was sponsored by Sir Macpherson Robertson, an Australian chocolate magnate, and offered a first prize of 10,000 English pounds — a big purse and a big race. The "racecourse" was 11,325 miles long.

Of a total of 64 entries, representing two dozen countries, only twenty planes actually took off when the race started on October 20. American hopefuls included a Northrup Delta, Monocoupe, Vance "Flying Wing," Lockheed Altair, a Bellanca tri-motor especially designed for long-distance air racing, and a Boeing 247D airliner. Among the others were the British-built Miles Falcon, Percival Gull, Fairy Fox, DH Leopard Moth and three new DH Comets, to name a few. Also entered were a French Bleriot 111-6, a Desoutter Mark II, and an Italian Bergamaschi PL-3, plus a Dutch airline Douglas DC-2. And, finally, the Gee Bee QED made it (by boat) to Mildenhall, England, just in time for the race.

The big Gee Bee, flown by Jackie Cochran and Wesley Smith, got only as far as Bucharest and was forced out with mechanical trouble. British Capt. Jim Mollison and his wife Amy led the race as far as Baghdad in one of the DH Comets. From there, a second Comet took over and remained in first position all the way to Melbourne. This plane, piloted by C. W. Scott and Thomas Black, averaged 180 mph to win. In second place was the Douglas DC-2, the Dutch entry, which arrived in Melbourne with a regular load of passengers. The third-place finisher was the Boeing 247D flown by Roscoe Turner and Clyde Pangborn. Cathart Jones, in the remaining DH Comet, was fourth. The

First postwar Thompson race (1946) went to Tex Johnston and his clipped-wing P-39 "Airacobra." (Leo Kohn Photo).

Tony LeVier's modified "Lightning" (P-38L-5) placed second in the 1946 Thompson. (Pete Bowers Photo).

Lockheed P-80 flown to 1st place in 1946 Thompson Jet Race by Maj. Gus Lundquist. (Steve Hudek Photo).

Jacqueline Cochran's "Mustang" (P-51C); second in '46 Bendix race at 420.925 mph. (Pete Bowers Photo).

Douglas A-26C, flown by Don Husted in 1946 Bendix race. (Leo Kohn Photo).

AT-6 (canopy modified), entered in Halle Trophy race for women. Marge Hurlbert was winner at 200.6 mph. (Leo Kohn Photo).

slower planes, judged on a handicap system, kept straggling into Melbourne for days afterwards.

THE 1935 NATIONAL AIR RACES, at Cleveland, August 30 to September 2, should have been called the "Ben Howard National Air Races" — Howard-built aircraft won the top five contests.

THE BENDIX TROPHY RACE, from Burbank to Cleveland, had eight starters. Six took off shortly after midnight, during the first minutes of September 2. The remaining pair, Jackie Cochran in a Northrup Gamma and Cecil Allen in Gee Bee #7, waited until 3 a.m. (Allen's Gee Bee was a composite of the salvaged remains of the Gee Bee R-1 and the R-2. It was very similar in appearance to these planes, though its fuselage was 2 feet longer and it had a rounded rudder resembling Bayles' Gee Bee Model Z).

Fog had rolled into Burbank between midnight and 3 a.m. when Cecil Allen began his take off run. Then, somewhere in the mist, near the end of the runway, he crashed to his death.

Jackie Cochran went behind a hangar and vomited, then returned to her plane and took off. She flew on instruments as far as the Arizona line but was turned back there by a violent squall line and an overheating engine.

Ben Howard, at the controls of his new cabin monoplane, Mr. Mulligan, and with Gordon Israel as co-pilot, flew into Cleveland a bare 23½ seconds ahead of Roscoe Turner. Ben and Gordon had flown above the weather, using oxygen. They landed in the rain at Cleveland with an average of 238.7 mph. Royal Leonard, in the Gee Bee QED, dropped out at Wichita.

THE GREVE TROPHY, again awarded to the pilot amassing the most points in a series of three races, went to Harold Neumann. Harold flew Howard's Mike to first place in all three races. His speeds were: 194.9, 207.2 and 212.7 mph. Roger Don Rae was second in Rudy Kling's Keith Rider.

THE THOMPSON TROPHY RACE was a heartbreaker for Roscoe Turner. Turner had lost the Bendix — by only 23½ seconds — to Howard's Mr. Mulligan. Then, in the Thompson, determined to scrooch Howard's cocky white monoplane, Turner flew a beautiful all-out race. He was well in the lead, with but 20 miles of the 150-mile race remaining, when his engine blew up.

Goodyear "Corsair" (F2G-1), with 4,000 hp swinging its prop, was flown by Cook Cleland to 1947 Thompson win. (Pete Bowers Photo).

Dick Becker's clipped-wing F2G-1, second in '47 Thompson. (Leo Kohn Photo).

Tony Janazzo crashed to his death during 7th lap of '47 Thompson in this F2G-1 "Corsair." (Pete Bowers Photo).

Jim Ruble took to his "rag bag" over Arizona when this P-38 caught fire during 1947 Bendix cross-country race. (Steve Hudek Photo).

Joe DeBona's P-51 racer; forced down in '48 Bendix; first place in '49 Bendix. (Leo Kohn Photo).

John Thomson's P-38 racer which placed 4th in the 1947 Sohio Trophy Race. (Leo Kohn Photo).

He landed safely — while Harold Neumann again piloted Mr. Mulligan to first place with an average of 220.2 mph. Steve Wittman, in Bonzo, was second at 218.6 mph and Roger Don Rae third with 213.9 mph.

THE WORLD'S LANDPLANE SPEED RECORD was raised again on September 13, when Jillionaire Howard Hughes flew his specially-built speed plane over a 3-kilometer (1.86 miles) course six times to average 352.39 mph. Thus the record was recovered from France again, because France's Raymond Delmotte had previously taken it from the U.S. with a speed of 314.32 mph.

Hughes also established a new transcontinental record in his H-1 Special. On January 19, 1937, he sped from Burbank to Newark at an average speed of 327.1 mph.

THE 1936 NATIONAL AIR RACES were held at Los Angeles, September 4-7, and therefore the Bendix was flown from east to west this year.

THE BENDIX TROPHY RACE, however, seemed more like a "Powder Puff Derby" than anything else. It was won by Louise Thaden and Blanche Noyes in a Staggerwing Beech (C-17R), at an average speed of 165.3 mph. Laura Ingalls was second in her Lockheed Orion at 157.5 mph. Bill Gulick placed third flying a Vultee V1A. Amelia Earhart did no better than fifth because of engine trouble with her new Lockheed Electra (the same plane in which she disappeared over the South Pacific). Lee Miles dropped out in the star-crossed Gee Bee QED; Ben Howard and his wife crash-landed in New Mexico, and Joe Jacobson suddenly found himself looking for his parachute rip-cord when his Northrup Gamma exploded and blew him from the cockpit. He found it — the rip-cord, that is.

THE GREVE TROPHY RACE was a single event this year, rather than the previous three heats. Michel Detroyat won it at 247 mph in his Caudron C-460. Development and construction of this airplane had been subsidized by the French Government, which caused some resentment among the U.S. pilots whose only "subsidies" were occasional free use of an engine from a manufacturer.

Harold Neumann, flying a new Folkerts Special, barely

Joe Ziegler's Curtiss P-40Q crashed during '47 Thompson. (Leo Kohn Photo).

P-63 Kingcobra, with A. T. Whiteside flying, competed in Tinnerman Trophy Races of 1947 and 1949. (Leo Kohn Photo).

Charles Tucker's Kingcobra; 2nd in '47 Tinnerman, 3rd in '49 Sohio and 5th in '49 Thompson. (Leo Kohn Photo).

squeezed by Art Chester to take second in the Greve race. Rudy Kling took fourth in the Keith Rider Suzy.

THE THOMPSON TROPHY RACE belonged to Detroyat throughout. The course was 15 laps — 150 miles — and he turned in a new high of 264.3 mph to win with a greater lead than any pilot before him. Earl Ortman, flying a new Keith Rider powered with a Wasp engine, was second at 248 mph. Roger Don Rae was third in a Menasco-powered Keith Rider. Lee Miles tried again in the Gee Bee QED with the usual result for that hard-luck machine.

THE 1937 NATIONAL AIR RACES, back at Cleveland once more, provided air racing with the two most exciting finishes in history. Rudy Kling beat Steve Wittman in the Greve race by approximately ¼-mile per hour. Rudy then compounded the felony by winning over Earl Ortman in the Thompson by a margin of 5/100-miles per hour — 256.91 against 256.86 mph!

THE BENDIX TROPHY RACE drew eight entries, six of whom finished. Perlick crashed his Staggerwing Beech on take off, and Joe Mackey, flying Turner's old Wedell-Williams, dropped out at St. Louis. Frank Fuller won with a new high of 258.2 mph in a Seversky P-35. Earl Ortman was second with 224.8 mph and Jackie Cochran third in a Staggerwing Beech.

THE GREVE TROPHY RACE, 10 laps for a total of 100 miles, had five entries, but the battle for first place was between Wittman and Kling all the way. At the finish it was Kling out front with a speed of 232.3 mph. Wittman's average was 232 mph. C. H. Gotch, in a modified Keith Rider, was third with 231.6 mph, having come up fast in the latter part of the race.

THE THOMPSON TROPHY RACE was undecided until the last split-second. Steve Wittman led most of the way but struck a bird, bending his prop, and fell back. Roscoe Turner then took over the lead. However, believing that he had missed a pylon, he turned to re-circle it and allowed Earl Ortman to blast into the number one spot. Earl, apparently thinking that he was fat, throttled back. He shouldn't have. Rudy Kling pushed everything to the firewall in his Folkerts and dived across the finish line to

Steve Wittman's P-63 in which he took 3rd in 1947 Tinnerman
race (Leo Kohn Photo).

Wittman "Buster," first place winner of 1947 Goodyear Trophy Race
—and many contests since. (Leo Kohn Photo).

Art Chester's Bonanza-tailed "Swee' Pea." Paul Penrose flew it to
2nd place in '47 Goodyear. (Leo Kohn Photo).

Fish Salmon piloted this Cosmic Wind racer to third place in 1947 Goodyear race. (Pete Bowers Photo).

Tony LeVier's Cosmic Wind was 4th in '47 Goodyear race. (Leo Kohn Photo).

Anson Johnson won '48 Thompson in this P-51 at 383.76 mph. (Steve Hudek Photo).

beat Ortman by approximately the length of his plane. It was a race the fans remembered.

THE WORLD'S LANDPLANE SPEED RECORD was bettered again on November 11, 1937, when Hermann Wurster flew 379.63 mph in a German Messerschmitt Bf.113R.

THE 1938 NATIONAL AIR RACES, at Cleveland, September 3-5, offered a total of $102,750 in prize money.

THE BENDIX TROPHY RACE had two new rules this year: blind flying instruments and radio were required for planes, and pilots had to be instrument-rated. Also, it was ruled that planes entered in the Bendix could not participate in the Thompson, although the pilots themselves could fly both contests.

Ten planes left Glendale, California, for Cleveland. Four were forced out along the way: Lee Gehlbach in a Wedell-Williams, Bob Perlick in a Staggerwing Beech, Frank Cordova flying the tri-motored Bellanca and George Armistead in the (you guessed it) Gee Bee QED. Bernarr McFadden cracked up his Northrup Gamma prior to the race.

Jackie Cochran won the Bendix in her new Seversky P-35 (civilian designation, SEV-S2) with an average speed of 249.74 mph. Frank Fuller, last year's winner, was second at 238.6 mph in an identical plane. Paul Mantz was third in a Lockheed Orion. All six finishers reported instrument weather conditions for the entire 2,043 miles of the race. Jackie, however, after a 15-minute gas stop at Cleveland, continued to Bendix, N. J., to establish a new women's west-east record 242.1 mph.

THE GREVE TROPHY RACE, 30 laps for 300 miles, produced another thrilling finish. Tony LeVier and Art Chester battled almost wing-to-wing—the lead often changing hands—throughout. LeVier finally took the checkered flag a few turns of the prop ahead of Chester. Their speeds were 250.9 and 250.4 mph respectively. Joe Jacobson was third in a new Keith Rider Eightball. Harry Crosby landed afire in the 14th lap.

THE THOMPSON TROPHY RACE, also 30 laps, 300 miles, attracted eight starters seeking a share of the $42,000 in prize money. And this race too would have been an extremely close one had Earl Ortman's engine not given trouble. As it was, Earl and Roscoe

Paul Mantz won '48 Bendix in this pea-green P-51. (Leo Kohn Photo).

Charles Walling was 3rd in '48 Sohio race flying this P-51. (Leo Kohn Photo).

1948 Goodyear winners in order that each finished. Pete Bowers Photo).

Fish Salmon's "Minnow," first in '48 Goodyear. (Pete Bowers Photo).

Steve Wittman in "Bonzo II" takes starter's flag in '48 Goodyear race. (Pete Bowers Photo).

Bill Brennand: small man—big pilot. (Leo Kohn Photo).

Turner—well out in front of the others—fought for the lead for 27 laps. Then, slowed by a broken oil line, Ortman fell back and Turner, who had held to a slim lead for 22 laps, went on to win with an average speed of 283.4 mph—a new record.

Ortman finished with an average of 269.7 mph—and a completely dry oil tank. His plane was the Keith Rider modified and now called the Marcoux-Bromberg. It was fitted with a 900-hp Wasp engine. Turner's plane, designed and built by Lawrence Brown, then modified by Matty Laird, had a 1,100-hp twin Wasp Senior in its nose. Steve Wittman was third and Leigh Wade fourth.

THE 1939 NATIONAL AIR RACES, September 2-5, were crowded off the front pages of the nation's newspapers by a declaration of war in Europe. These were to be the last Nationals for the duration. Earlier, on March 30, Luftwaffe Capt. H. Dieterle had flown a Heinkel HE-112U to a new landplane speed record of 463.92; and on April 26, Fritz Wendel upped this mark to 469.22 mph in an ME-109R.

THE BENDIX TROPHY RACE was again won by Frank Fuller in his Seversky P-35—the prototype of the famed P-47 Thunderbolt. Fuller's average speed was 282.1 mph, another Bendix record. He continued to Bendix, N. J., after stopping at Cleveland to also up the record from Burbank to Bendix. Art Bussy, flying the tri-motored Bellanca 28-92, was second at 244.5 mph, and Paul Mantz placed third in his Lockheed Orion.

THE GREVE TROPHY RACE was 20 laps for 200 miles this year. It turned into a one-man show after the half-way mark was reached, for Art Chester was virtually alone on the race-course by then. Lee Williams, in the Brown Miss Los Angeles, crashed to his death at the scattering pylon. Tony LeVier was forced down with mechanical trouble in the 11th lap; and Harry Crosby was flagged down by officials when, after 13 laps, he still could not retract his landing gear. Chester, piloting his sleek Goon, could have coasted to a sure win at almost any speed he chose. Characteristically, he chose the highest speed he could coax from his craft. He finished with a new Greve record of 263.4 mph.

THE 1939 THOMPSON TROPHY RACE, another 300-miler, had seven

1949 Halle Trophy Race for women was limited to stock AT-6's. Above, Dot Lemon and her plane. Grace Harris was winner. (Leo Kohn Photo).

Stub-winged F2G-1 "Corsair" in which Cook Cleland won 1949 Thompson. (Leo Kohn Photo).

Ben McKillen flew this F2G-1 to first in the '49 Tinnerman and 3rd in the '49 Thompson. (Pete Bowers Photo).

entries. Roscoe Turner, flying his Brown-Laird, again had pylon trouble; but he circled the missed marker and then worked his way into the lead on the ninth lap. Tony LeVier, who had led since the fifth circuit of the course, remained in second place and he and Turner crossed the finish line in that order; Turner with an average of 282.5 mph and LeVier with a speed of 272.5 mph. Art Chester dropped out with engine trouble, and Earl Ortman took over the number three position and finished there. Harry Crosby was fourth.

The year 1939 also gave a brief moment of glory to the last of the Gee Bees, the big QED, a plane that seemed born to trouble. On May 24, Mexican speed pilot Francisco Sarabia flew the QED from Mexico City to New York in 10 hours and 47 minutes—a non-stop record for the 2,350 miles. But two weeks later the QED, as if weary of it all after having finally proven itself, plunged into the Potomac River and took the life of Francisco Sarabia.

THE 1946 NATIONAL AIR RACES, back at the same old stand in Cleveland, were held from August 30 to September 2. The planes were all WW II surplus fighters. This resulted in plenty of speed but, paradoxically, it soon became evident that speed alone was not what the public had been paying to see. Somehow, the average spectator just couldn't work up the enthusiasm over a big mass-produced military plane that he could when rooting for, say, one of Ben Howard's presumptuous little homebuilts. Nevertheless, the Mustangs and Cobras and Cosairs provided the fans with the fastest, hairiest, closed-course air races ever held. This era too—'46 through '49—was a time for giants.

THE BENDIX TROPHY RACE, from Van Nuys, California, to Cleveland, had 22 starters and 15 finishers. The first four places were claimed by pilots flying modified P-51's. Paul Mantz was first with an average speed of 435.5 mph. Jackie Cochran drove her #13 P-51B into Cleveland with an average speed of 420.925 mph. Tom Mayson was third. A Douglas A-26, flown by Don Husted, was sixth. A special Bendix for jets was won by Col. Leon Gray, flying a Lockheed P-80. His speed was 494.7 mph.

THE 1946 THOMPSON TROPHY RACE consisted of 10 laps for a total distance of 300 miles. (This was another thing the paying customers didn't like about the post-war races. As speed increased,

Bill Odom crashed to his death in "Beguine" during the 1949 Thompson race. (Leo Kohn Photo).

Don Bussart had engine trouble with his DH "Mosquito" in 1949 Bendix, placed 4th. (Leo Kohn Photo).

Republic AT-12, flown by Vince Perron in '49 Bendix. (Steve Hudek Photo).

106

James Harp's P-39, a 1949 Sohio entry. (Leo Kohn Photo).

J. H. G. McArthur could manage only 3rd place in the '49 Tinnerman with his Supermarine "Spitfire" XIV. (Leo Kohn Photo).

1949 Goodyear winners. Argandar Special—later, "Deerfly"—in foreground was 2nd; "Buster" (center) placed 1st and "Bonzo" was 3rd. (Pete Bowers Photo).

so did the distances between pylons, and no longer could the fans witness at close range an entire race). Twelve planes lined up for the race-horse start, and Alvin "Tex" Johnston in a clipped-wing P-39Q took the lead from the beginning. For a time Johnston was harassed by George Welch in a P-51, but after Welch dropped out Tex had no trouble in maintaining his lead until the finish. His average speed was 373.9 mph, a new record. Tony LeVier was second in a P-38. Earl Ortman probably felt right at home in third place—he had placed second or third in the last four Thompsons that preceded the war.

Major Gus Lundquist, in a P-80, won the Thompson Jet Race at 515.9 mph.

THE SOHIO TROPHY RACE, flown for the first time this year, drew entries from the overflow that had failed to qualify for the Thompson (the Thompson was limited to the 12 fastest qualifiers). And while this contest was open to 12 participants also, only 7 actually started. Dale Fulton took first place in a P-51D. His speed was 352.78 mph. Bill Ong was second, also in a Mustang.

THE 1947 NATIONAL AIR RACES packed a lot of excitement into just three days of racing—August 30 to September 1. The wildest Thompson of all was flown this year; a number of new records were established, and a significant new event was introduced.

THE GOODYEAR TROPHY RACE, guaranteed by the Goodyear Tire & Rubber Company for three years, was limited to planes with stock engines of 190-cubic-inches displacement or less. Further rules, aimed at promoting safe designs, rather definitely pinned down general specifications and sound construction techniques. Thus the midgets were born, and the "little guy" was assured a place in the air racing business.

Art Chester's new *Swee' Pea,* flown by Paul Penrose, qualified fastest at 167 mph (all these little craft were powered with Continental 85 engines), but Bill Brennand, in the Wittman *Buster,* barely squeezed by *Swee' Pea* to win the first Goodyear at 165.857 mph. *Swee' Pea's* average was 165.393 mph. Herman "Fish" Salmon was third in his Cosmic Wind *Minnow.*

THE BENDIX TROPHY RACE, from Van Nuys to Cleveland, had 12 entries. Paul Mantz won again, with a new record of 460.4 mph,

Vince Ast was 4th in '49 Goodyear flying "Ballerina." (Pete Bowers Photo).

Al Foss' "Jinny" dropped out of the '49 Goodyear in 12th lap. Later rebuilt by Jim Dewey; flown by Mike Dewey, and renamed "Little Mike." (Leo Kohn Photo).

Reaver Special first appeared in 1948 races. It was built by Nicholas-Beazley team. (Leo Kohn Photo).

#34 is Williams "Estrellita"; #92, Falck "Rivets"; #35, Coonley Special; #29, L. I. T. "Chappy." (Pete Bowers Photo).

Long "Peashooter," placed 4th in '49 Continental Motors race at Miami. Top speed about 220 mph. (Pete Bowers Photo).

Lazor-Rautenstrauch, originally "Bell of Bethany," rebuilt and now known as "Pogo." (Don Wigton Photo).

in his red P-51. Joe DeBona was but 78 seconds behind. The first six finishers were *Mustangs*. Jim Ruble left his P-38, high over Arizona, when it caught fire.

The Jet Bendix was again won by Col. Leon Gray in his P-80, with an average speed of 507.3 mph.

THE KENDALL OIL TROPHY RACE, a special event for *Mustangs*, was taken by Steve Beville in a P-51D. His speed was 384.6 mph. Kendall Everson was second in an A-36, and Woody Edmonson third in a P-51A.

THE TINNERMAN TROPHY RACE was for Bell P-63 *Kingcobras*. Top prize money in this one was captured by Ken Knight—at a speed of 352.168 mph—in a P-63A. Charles Tucker was second in a P-63C-5, and Steve Wittman third, also in a C-5 Model.

THE HALLE TROPHY RACE FOR WOMEN, limited to stock AT-6's was won by Ruth Johnson at 223.4 mph.

THE ALLISON JET TROPHY RACE, a round trip from Cleveland to Indianapolis and back, saw Capt. Dick Burnor in first place with a speed of 494.3 mph. Capt. E. Bishop was second. All six entries were Lockheed P-80A's.

THE SOHIO TROPHY RACE was for Lockheed *Lightnings*. Seven started and five finished, with Tony LeVier in the number one slot at 360.866 mph. Charles Walling was second.

THE THOMPSON TROPHY RACE, limited to 12 planes, had 13. A P-40 —that's right, a P-40—flown by one Joe Ziegler who, of course, had not qualified, somehow lined up and took off in the race-horse start with the legal entries. But he should have "stood in bed." Ziegler bailed out in the 13th lap and broke his leg after his engine quit.

Three other pilots dropped out with dead engines: Jack Hardwick—who landed wheels-up, tore a wing off his P-51 and jumped from the burning wreckage without a scratch—Charles Walling (down in one piece), and Woody Edmundson, who crash-landed and was pulled from his burning plane injured, though not fatally.

Tony Jannazo was not as fortunate. In the seventh lap, he flew into the ground at 400 mph. Then, after Paul Penrose was forced down, there were suddenly but 7 planes left in the race.

Denight "DDT," began career in 1949 and has since raced at Miami, Reading, Detroit, and Dansville, N. Y. Top speed is about 230 mph. (Steve Hudek Photo).

Pitts "Li'l Monster" designed and built by Curtiss Pitts, was flown to 4th place in '51 Detroit races. (Steve Hudek Photo).

"Mammy," a Dave Long design built by Curtiss Pitts and owned by Luther Johnson of Greenville, S. C. (Marvin Border Photo).

Finally, Ron Puckett, in fourth position, had something come unstuck in the big Wasp Major engine in his *Corsair*—just one lap from the end—and Cook Cleland, who had led from the fourth lap, showed the way over the finish line to the five remaining racers. Cleland's speed was 396.131 mph, a new closed-course record, and he collected $19,500 for his trouble. Dick Becker, flying a Goodyear-built *Corsair* (F2G-1) identical to the winning ship, and also owned by Cleland, was second. Jay Demming was third in a Bell P-39Q-10.

THE 1948 NATIONAL AIR RACES had little to offer in the Bendix or Thompson. The war-surplus fighters were speedy, and fancy paint jobs helped give them the appearance of racers, but the fans were fast taking a ho-hum attitude toward them. The military jets generated even less enthusiasm among the spectators.

It was the little Goodyear racers—the homebuilts that could polish pylons around a racecourse contained within the airport boundaries—that captured the affection and imagination of the crowd. Twenty-four "little 'uns" showed up, including most of those that had flown in the first Goodyear—slicked up and already modified here and there—plus nearly a dozen new ones.

THE GOODYEAR TROPHY RACE consisted of four heat races, a couple of semi-finals; the final, and even a consolation race. Qualifying trials were run to determine starting position, and Art Chester, in *Swee' Pea* (with a new Y-tail this year), turned in the fastest average speed of 180 mph. In the finals, however, *Swee' Pea* did no better than third. Fish Salmon, in his Cosmic Wind *Minnow*, (greatly altered from its configuration of the previous year), swept to first place and Steve Wittman was second in a new Wittman Special. Bill Brennand took fourth in the Wittman *Buster*.

THE BENDIX TROPHY RACE, from Long Beach, California to Cleveland, was won by Paul Mantz in his pea-green P-51. It was Paul's third win of this classic, and he managed it with an average speed of 448 mph. Linton Carney was second at 446.1 mph. and fabulous Jackie was right on Carney's tail in her P-51 with an average speed of 445.8 mph. Jessee Stallings made it to Cleveland in his DH *Mosquito* on one fan; and Joe DeBona ran out of gas almost within spittin' distance of the Cleveland Airport.

The Jet Bendix was flown by six Navy FJ-1's (a sea-going ver-

"Beetle Bomb," built by Alvin Anderson of Elmhurst, Ill., has diamond-shaped fuselage; 15-ft. span. (Leo Kohn Photo).

Veteran "Bonzo" is still winning races; a regular contender at the Ft. Wayne Championship events. (Pete Bowers Photo).

"Deerfly," finished in the money at '58 Ft. Wayne races; in last place at 1960 Ft. Wayne Championship. Piloted by Jim Williams and Mel Stickney. (Don Wigton Photo).

"Tater Chip," designed by Ned Kensinger of Ft. Worth, crashed during 1960 Ft. Wayne race killing Jim Rice. (Leo Kohn Photo).

Bill Falck's "Rivets," (original configuration) first raced in '48. 1st in '58 Central New York races; 2nd in 1959 Fort Wayne finals. (Leo Kohn Photo).

"Mr. Zip," as it appeared at the 1958 Central New York Air Races at Fulton. (Steve Hudek Photo).

sion of the F-86), and Ens. F. E. Brown was the first to Cleveland with an average speed of 489.5 mph.

THE TINNERMAN TROPHY RACE was open to everything except the F2G *Corsairs.* The F2G's were eliminated by restricting the race to engines of 2,850 cubic inches or less. These craft (only 13 were built near the end of the war) were powered with the 28-cylinder Pratt and Whitney Wasp Major—a buzz-box capable of producing 4,000-hp!

Bruce Raymond was first around the 7-lap 15-mile course in a P-51D, with a speed of 362.2 mph. Bob Euker was next, in a P-63A, at 362.1 mph.

THE SOHIO TROPHY RACE was a handicap event this year. Bob Euker won it at 320.2 mph.

THE KENDALL TROPHY RACE was for the ladies, and Grace Harris flew her AT-6 to a new record of 235 mph.

THE ALLISON TROPHY RACE FOR JETS, Cleveland to Indianapolis and back, went to Lt. L. Thompson in an FJ-1 *Fury.* His winning speed was 490 mph.

THE 1948 THOMPSON TROPHY RACE lost seven of the ten starting planes to engine trouble. The last to drop out was Charles Brown flying *Cobra II.* Brown was well in the lead, and on the way to a new all-time Thompson record, when his engine gave out on the next-to-last lap. Anson Johnson went on to win, averaging 383.8 in a P-51D. Second was Bruce Raymond.

THE 1949 NATIONAL AIR RACES added new records to almost every event. This year also saw the last of the WW II fighters converted to racers. Air racing in the years ahead would belong to the midgets.

THE BENDIX TROPHY RACE was flown with a race-horse start from Rosamond Dry Lake, California. Three *Mustangs,* a DH *Mosquito,* a B-26 and a Republic AT-12 made up the field. They arrived in Cleveland in that order—except for Vincent Perron in the AT-12, who dropped out enroute. Joe DeBona was first with a time of 4 hours, 16 minutes and 17½ seconds; his average speed, 470.136 mph. Stan Reaver was second and Fish Salmon third.

Major Vernon Ford took first place in the Jet Bendix, flying

Garland Pack's "Johnny Reb," crashed during 1960 Ft. Wayne race after mid-air collision with "Tater Chip." Charlie Bishop died in "Johnny Reb," Jim Rice in "Tater Chip." (Don Wigton Photo).

"Shoestring," designed by Rod Kreimendahl and built by Ast Bros., of Van Nuys, is pictured here at 1959 Ft. Wayne races. (Steve Hudek Photo).

Leighnor Special "Mirage," a steady contender at Ft. Wayne, though never a winner. Now owned by Howard Hutches of Orlando, Fla. (Steve Hudek Photo).

his Air Force F-84E to Cleveland in 3 hours, 45 minutes and 51 seconds, to average 529.6-mph. And Lt. Walt Rew won the Allison Jet Trophy, flying between Indianapolis and Cleveland at 594.8 mph in an F-80C.

THE SOHIO TROPHY RACE, with nine starters, was led by Bill Odom from the third lap. His winning speed was 388 mph. His *Mustang* had been greatly modified, its underslung belly radiator having been removed and replaced by wingtip radiators.

THE KENDALL TROPHY RACE FOR WOMEN was again taken by Grace Harris, who averaged 216.7 mph in a stock AT-6.

THE TINNERMAN TROPHY RACE was easily gobbled up by Ben Mc-Killen's big F2G-1 *Corsair*. Ben led all the way and averaged 386.069 mph. Wilson Newhall was second in a P-51 and J. H. G. McArthur third in a British *Spitfire*.

THE THOMPSON TROPHY RACE, reduced to a total distance of 225 miles this year, was open to the ten fastest qualifiers. The top qualifying speed was Dick Becker's 414 mph; but Dick burned up the engine in his *Corsair* doing it and his place was taken by Ron Puckett in another F2G.

Favored to win were Cook Cleland in his well-muscled F2G, and Bill Odom in his P-51 *Beguine;* but it was all over by the end of the second lap. Odom went into a high-speed stall and crashed into a house killing himself, a mother, and her son. Cleland's lead was never challenged. His winning speed of 397.071-mph was a new record—perhaps the last one for the big racers. A growing public apathy toward the war surplus craft, plus the deaths of two innocent people, combined to bring an end to the big, unlimited-class of closed-course racers.

THE GOODYEAR TROPHY RACE was a different story. The small racers, flying their trials and races directly in front of the spectators, provided constant thrills in one fiercely-contested heat after another—yet did so with a degree of sanity and safety. Steve Wittman led the heat winners with an average of 184 mph, but, in the 12-lap final, it was Bill Brennand, flying Wittman's *Buster*, who romped in with first money. Bill's speed was 177.34 mph; his prize: $7,000. Keith Sorensen was second in *Deerfly* and Steve Wittman placed third in *Bonzo II*. Steve, a fine pilot and a top engineer, developed the spring-steel landing gear now featured on stock Cessnas. He has also invented special racing propellers and was flying laminar-flow airfoils years before they were announced by the N.A.C.A.

THE SAN DIEGO GOLD CUP RACE, April 24, 1949, took the life of Art Chester when his *Swee' Pea II* went into a high speed stall during the second heat. In the first heat, Bob Heisel, flying the Pitts *Pellet,* crashed to his death apparently from the same cause. Her man "Fish" Salmon took first place in his Cosmic wind *Minnow* with a speed of 175.27. Steve Wittman in *Bonzo* was right behind with 175 mph, and Bob Downey next in *Ballerina* with an average of 174 mph.

THE 1950 MIAMI AIR MANEUVERS featured a 12-lap 24-mile event for small racers sponsored by Continental Motors. Steve Wittman took top money in *Bonzo* at 185.4 mph. Keith Sorensen in *Ballerina,* Bob Downey in *Shoestring,* and Phil Quigley in the Pitts *Li'l Monster* finished in that order. This race, and a similar one at Detroit, more or less replaced the Nationals which were not held this year.

THE 1950 DETROIT AIR FAIR had as its main event a 12-lap 24 mile midget race—again Continental sponsored—that went to John Jones when he ate up the course in the Cosmic Wind *Little Toni* at the rate of 187.785 mph. Steve Wittman was two miles per hour slower in *Bonzo II.* Keith Sorensen was next in *Deerfly,* followed by Kip Mone in *Estrellita.*

THE TENNESSEE PRODUCTS CUP RACE at Chattanooga, May 20, 1951, was the setting for the first mid-air race collision when Bob Porter, flying *Buster,* shoved his wheels through the top of the wing on the Pack *Johnny Reb* being piloted by Joe Mangano. Porter finished the race and Mangano got down safely. Steve Wittman collected first money with 178.3 mph.

THE 1951 NATIONAL AIR RACES, held at Detroit, August 18 and 19, actually had but one closed-course event to offer the paying customers—the Continental Motors Trophy for midgets. Otherwise, the "National Air Races" was a military air show.

A lone F-86 flew around the old Thompson course for the "Thompson Trophy." An assortment of bombers and fighter planes flew a Bendix Trophy Race of sorts, and the jets did a

Ohm Special, designed by airline pilot Dick Ohm, flew at 1959 Ft. Wayne meet, has recently been re-worked and now has "Mustang"-type rudder. (Steve Hudek Photo).

Jim Kistler's "La Jollita," was designed by Lockheed Engineer Bill Statler. (Leo Kohn Photo).

"Miss Dara" (Dayton Air Racing Association), a newcomer that will be a real threat in the sixties. (Photo: Don Berliner).

few other things—sometimes even in view of the spectators—but they didn't race.

(This is not intended as a slap at the Navy or Air Force. A mighty secure feeling can result from the sound of a pair of jet fighter types screaming away in the dead of night to investigate an unidentified radar blip—and no one can deny that the SAC has kept the Soviets in more or less peaceful frustration for lo these many years. But the military jets were not designed for air racing; and a plane that requires 15 miles to make a 360-degree turn can hardly be expected to be popular with racing fans).

THE CONTINENTAL MOTORS RACE consisted of 15 laps around a 2½-mile course for a total of 37½ miles. John Jones again placed first, this time in *Shoestring*, and established a new record of 197.2 mph. Steve Wittman was second and Keith Sorensen third —exactly the same order in which they had finished the Detroit races a year previously.

THE 1952 TENNESSEE PRODUCTS CUP RACE, at Chattanooga on May 18, produced plenty of thrills for the 65,000 fans when new-comer Bill Falck, flying *Rivets,* edged out the old master, Steve Wittman, by 16/100ths mph for first place. Falck got off slowly then chipped away at Steve's lead until lap 8. From that point it was a wild 7-lap battle to the finish line. According to Don Berliner, PRPA official, Bill Falck was the happiest winner to ever take the checkered flag. Bob Porter was third and Bill Brennand fourth.

THE 1952 CONTINENTAL MOTORS TROPHY RACE, at Detroit, August 30-September 1, turned into another hairy contest, this time between Steve Wittman and John P. Jones. Jones, refusing to accept Steve's lead, did everything but beat his *Shoestring* with a stick—rolling his wheels on the straight-aways and kicking up dust with his wingtip vortices on turns—but not only lost to Steve by 13/100 mph, was also disqualified for "extremely low flying" to boot. Steve's speed was 197.29 mph. Jones' average was 197.16 Bill Falck was second.

THE 1954 DANSVLLE, NEW YORK AIR RACES, flown July 4, intro-duced another newcomer to the winner's spot. Jim Miller, flying

Latest configuration of Bill Falck's "Rivets," a racer with "winning ways." (Photo: Leo Kohn).

Tom Cassutt's Cassutt Special I, now known as the "Jersey Skeeter." (Leo Kohn Photo).

Jim Miller's "Little Gem," first place in '59 and '60 Ft. Wayne National Air Races. (Don Berliner Photo).

Miller's *Little Gem,* led a field of eleven to win at 181.06 mph. Dick Ohm was second in *Shoestring.* Bill Falck, the top qualifier, was eliminated for cutting a pylon. However, the consnsus was that a rookie judge goofed. Characteristically, Bill Falck accepted the ruling without complaint. (No air races were held in 1953).

THE 1955 FRANK E. GANNETT TROPHY RACE, at Dansville, N.Y. July 3, was a repeat of the '52 Chattanooga contest between Steve Wittman and Bill Falck. Bill's *Rivets* again beat out Steve's *Bonzo* by the proverbial mosquito's whisker: 186.85 versus 185.33 mph. Dick Ohm in *Shoestring* was third and Tom Cassutt gave an indication of things to come by copping the number four slot in his new Cassutt Special I.

THE 1956 SPRINGFIELD, ILLINOIS, AIR RACES, held May 27 logged Falck's third win over Wittman and again it was close: 191.07 against 190.02 mph. Tom Cassutt took third in this relatively small event with an average of 188.77 mph.

THE 1956 FRANK E. GANNETT TROPHY RACE was held at Niagara Falls, N.Y., July 8. This race was a play-back of the Springfield contest a few weeks before, although the speeds were up: Falck, Wittman and Cassutt in that order, with averages of 199.96, 199.15 and 197.62 mph. John Scoville crashed in front of the stands and, though seriously injured, recovered.

THE 1956 S. J. WITTMAN TROPHY RACE, held at Oshkosh, Wisconsin, August 5, saw the Wittman-Falck feud continue, but Steve was unbeatable on his home grounds and managed to edge out Bill by 8/10 of a second for first place. Their speeds were 196.84 and 196.72 mph! Dick Ohm and Charlie Bishop were next in line at the money-window.

THE 1957 S. J. WITTMAN TROPHY RACE, at Oshkosh, August 11, afforded Steve Wittman a breather. Tom Cassutt had not yet perfected his racing technique, and Bill Falck's *Rivets,* damaged in a hangar fire, had just been rebuilt and was not thoroughly tested. Steve's average was 192.76 mph. Tom Cassutt in his Cassutt Special placed second with 187.04, and Bill Falck finished with 186.39 mph. Mel Stickney's smooth control-handling failed to make up for *Mammy's* lack of speed.

Pack "Li'l Rebel," always a bridesmaid but never a bride; never far behind the winner, but so far unable to win. (Leo Kohn Photo)

Fuselage modification stretched-out this Cosmic Wind, but results were disappointing. (Pete Bowers Photo).

Mel Stickney and de-jugged "Lil' Rebel." Mel's regular job is that of pilot for Pan Am. He flies DC-8's (to which he refers as "flying IBM machines") to Europe. Mel has also raced automobiles and boats.

THE 1957 FORT WAYNE INDUSTRIES TROPHY RACE, at Ft. Wayne, Ind., September 1, produced no upsets. It put Bill Falck back in the driver's seat with another fraction-of-a-mile-per-hour win over Steve Wittman—196.65 versus 196.29—with Cassutt again in the third slot. Charlie Bishop flew *Johnny Reb* to fourth place and Dick Ohm was fifth—barely 4/100 mph behind Charlie.

THE 1958 FORT WAYNE INDUSTRIES TROPHY RACE, held August 31, provided Tom Cassutt with the opportunity to finally complete his climb to the top. His Cassutt Special led Wittman and Falck—flying their usual split-second-apart—by a decisive two miles per hour at the finish line. This contest had a total of 14 entries. Cassutt's speed was 195.8 mph. Wittman averaged 193.9 in *Bonzo*, and Falck's *Rivets* was credited with 193.15 mph. Jim Miller in *Little Gem* was fourth and Mel Stickney fifth in *Li'l Rebel*.

THE 1959 FORT WAYNE RACES, on September 20, produced a new champion. Jim Miller hit his stride in his slick *Little Gem* and placed first with an average of 199.15 mph. The old order was dethroned (though Bill Falck was second at 196.94) and Paul Booth flew the new Pack *Grey Ghost* to third place first time out. Tom Cassutt, in a new Cassutt Special II was fourth. Miller established a new qualifying record of 209.56 mph.

THE 1960 FORT WAYNE RACES, held July 4, brought the first fatal accident to midget competition since 1950. It was a double tragedy resulting from a mid-air collision between Charlie Bishop, in the Pack *Johnny Reb*, and Jim Rice flying *Tater Chip*. The accident occurred on the way to the scattering pylon.

The race itself, consisting of the usual three heats, was the fastest ever. Jim Miller's *Little Gem* took the second heat with 207.27 mph. Bill Falck, in *Rivets*, averaged 205.24 in this same heat. This pair finished in this order, with final averages of 200.23 and 198.89 mph respectively. Mel Stickney, in *Deerfly*, was sixth at 187.8, a speed that would have put him in top money only a few years before. Jan Christie, a Norwegian pilot who flew the Cassutt Special II to fifth place, was the first non-national ever to race a midget in the U.S.A.

THE 1961 FORT WAYNE AIR RACES were held on July 1—according to the Ft. Wayne Chamber of Commerce. But no racing planes participated. Of course, it's possible to have a race between stock lightplanes—Pipers, Cessnas, etc. — but the Professional Race Pilots Association does not officially recognize that any race was held in 1961 in the U.S., at Ft. Wayne or elsewhere.

THE 1962 FORT RUCKER, ALABAMA, AIR RACES, scheduled for July 14, were cancelled at the last minute. Demonstration races, contests in which no prize money was awarded, were held in 1962 at Rockford, Illinois, during the annual Experimental Aircraft Association fly-in and, later, at Huntington, Indiana. There was no other air racing of consequence in the U.S. during 1962. The following assessment of the current racing scene is from Don Berliner of the Professional Race Pilots Association:

"The future of air racing in the U.S. is, at best, gloomy. For the past decade the sport has managed to keep from dying, but little more. Though at times there appeared cause for hope, the needed financial backing never arrived.

"As far as spectators and participants are concerned, there are enough of both to warrant continued activity. Unfortunately, this is not the entire story. Sponsoring and promoting groups— without which there can be no significant amount of racing— cannot be found.

"But thanks to the support of the Experimental Aircraft Association (EAA), there are more racers being built today than at any time since the late 1940's. And I believe that one major national race could attract sufficient attention to get the sport back on its feet.

"Of the 100-plus midget racers built, a large number are in flying shape or could be readied on short notice if the right airport (minimum of traffic, yet near a population center) and a promoter willing to take on the job were found.

"Aside from the midgets, the only all-out closed-course air racing done today is in England, where Cessnas, Pipers, Austers and homebuilt Turbulents compete for numerous trophies, including the famous King's Cup in the annual National Air Races. While these races are of the handicap type, there seems to be developing some interest in one-design class racing with homebuilts. This could be picked up in the U.S.

"Though the outlook is dim, there are still those who go right ahead and build new racers, confident that someone will put on a race. Until now, they have been correct—let's hope that they continue to be."

Pilot	Aircraft	hp	Speed	

INTERNATIONAL BENNETT CUP

1909

Pilot	Aircraft	hp	Speed	
1. Curtiss	Curtiss Golden Flyer	50	47.65	mph
2. Bleriot	Bleriot XI	60	46.83	
3. Latham	Antoinette	50	42.50	
4. Lefebvre	Wright	25	35.7	

1910

1. Grahame-White	Bleriot XI	100	61	
2. Moisant	Bleriot XI	50	31.5	
3. Ogilvie	Wright "C"	35	29.4	
4. Latham	Antoinette	100		

1911

1. Weyman	Nieuport	100	78	
2. Leblanc	Bleriot	100	75.8	
3. Nieuport	Nieuport	70	75.07	
4. Ogilvie	Baby Wright	50	53.3	

1912

1. J. Vedrines	Deperdussin	160	105.5	
2 Prevost	Deperdussin	100	103.8	
3. Frey	Hanriot	100		

1913

1. Prevost	Deperdussin	160	124.5	
2. E. Vedrines	Ponnier	160	123	
3. Gilbert	Deperdussin	160	119.5	
4. Crombez	Deperdussin	160	106.9	

1920

1. Sadi-Lecointe	Nieuport	320	168.5	mph
2. de Romanet	Spad	320	113.5	
Schroeder	Verville-Packard	638		
Rinehart	Dayton-Wright	250		
Rohlfs	Texas Wildcat	435		

INTERNATIONAL SCHNEIDER TROPHY RACE

1913

1. Prevost	Deperdussin	160	45.75	mph
2. Weyman	Nieuport	160		

1914

1. Pixton	Sopwith Tabloid	100	86.7	mph
2. Burri	FBA Flying Boat	100	62	

1920

1. Bologna	Savoia S-12	500	107.2	mph

1921

1. Briganti	Macchi M-7	250	117.8	mph
Zanetti	Macchi M-19	720		

Pilot	Aircraft	hp	Speed	
	1922			
1. Baird	Supermarine Sea Lion	450	145.7	mph
2. Passaleva	Savoia S-51	300	143.5	
3. Zanetti	Macchi M-17	250	133	
4. Cornolino	Macchi M-7	250	90.6	
	1923			
1. Rittenhouse	Navy Curtiss R-3	465	177.38	mph
2. Irvine	Navy Curtiss R-3	465	173.46	
3. Baird	Supermarine Sea Lion	575	157.17	
Wead	Navy Wright NW-2	700		
	1925			
1. Doolittle	Army Curtiss R3C-2	620	232.57	mph
2. Broad	Gloster III	700	199.16	
3. de Briganti	Macchi M-33	435	168.4	
Cuddihy	Navy Curtiss R3C-2	620		
Ofstie	Navy Curtiss R3C-2	620		
	1926			
1. de Bernardi	Macchi M-39	800	246.496	mph
2. Schilt	Curtiss R3C-2	620	231.36	
3. Bacula	Macchi M-39	800	218	
4. Tomlinson	Navy Curtiss F6C-1	435	136.9	
Cuddihy	Navy Curtiss R3C-4	700		
	1927			
1. Webster	Supermarine S-5	875	281.65	mph
2. Worsley	Supermarine S-5	875	273.07	
Guazzetti	Macchi M-52	1030		
Kinkead	Gloster IV	875		
de Bernardi	Macchi M-52	1030		
	1929			
1. Waghorn	Supermarine S-6	1900	328.63	mph
2. Dal Molin	Macchi M-52	1030	284.2	
3. d'Arcy Greig	Supermarine S-5	875	282.1	
Atcherly	Supermarine S-6	1900		
Cadringher	Macchi M-67	1400		
Monti	Macchi M-67	1400		
	1931			
1. Boothman	Supermarine S-6B	2350	340.1	mph

	1920			
1. Mosely	Verville-Packard	638	156.5	mph
2. Hartney	Thomas-Morse MB-3	300	148	
3. Acosta	Ansaldo Balilla	220	134.5	
4. St. Clair Street	Orenco D	300	133	
5. Laverents	Vought VE-7	180	125	
6. Roullot	DH-4	400	124	
Kirby	SE-5A	180		

Pilot	Aircraft	hp	Speed
1921			
1. Acosta	Navy Curtiss R-1	400	176.7 mph
2. Coombs	Cactus Kitten triplane	435	170.2
3. Macready	Thomas-Morse MB-6	400	160.7
4. Bertaud	Ansaldo Balilla	400	149.7
Hartney	Thomas-Morse MB-7	400	
1922			
1. Maughan	Army Curtiss R-6	460	205.8 mph
2. Maitland	Army Curtiss R-6	460	198.8
3. Brow	Navy Curtiss R-2	400	193.2
4. Williams	Navy Curtiss R-1	400	188
5. Barksdale	Verville-Sperry R-3	380	181
1923			
1. Williams	Navy Curtiss R2C-1	500	243.67 mph
2. Brow	Navy Curtiss R2C-1	500	241.78
3. Sanderson	Navy Wright F2W	700	230.06
4. Callaway	Navy Wright F2W	700	230
5. Miller	Army Curtiss R-6	500	218.9
1924			
1. Mills	Verville-Sperry R-3	500	215.72 mph
2. Brookley	Army Curtiss R-6	500	214.75
3. Stoner	Curtiss Hawk PW-8A	460	167.9
Skeel	Army Curtiss R-6	500	
1925			
1. Bettis	Army Curtiss R3C-1	620	248.975 mph
2. Williams	Navy Curtiss R3C-1	620	241.695
3. Dawson	Curtiss Hawk P-1	435	169.9
4. Norton	Curtiss Hawk PW-8	460	168.8

THOMPSON TROPHY RACE

Pilot	Aircraft	hp	Speed
1929*			
1. Davis	Travel Air Model R	400	194.9 mph
2. Breene	Curtiss Hawk P-3A	450	186.8
3. Turner	Lockheed Vega	450	163.8
			* Thompson Cup
1930			
1. Holman	Laird Solution	450	201.91 mph
2. Haizlip	Travel Air Model R	400	199.8
3. Howard	Howard *Pete*	90	162.8
4. Adams	Travel Air biplane	300	142.6
1931			
1. Bayles	Gee Bee Model Z	535	236.239 mph
2. Wedell	Wedell-Williams	535	227.99
3. Jackson	Laird Solution	525	211.18
4. Hall	Gee Bee Model Y	450	201.25
5. Eaker	Lockheed Altair	550	196.83
6. Howard	Howard *Pete*	90	163.57
7. Ong	Laird Speedwing	350	153.05
Doolittle	Laird Super Solution	535	

Pilot	*Aircraft*	*hp*	*Speed*
	1932		
1. Doolittle	Gee Bee R-1	800	252.686 mph
2. Wedell	Wedell-Williams	535	242.49
3. Turner	Wedell-Williams	535	233.04
4. Haizlip	Wedell-Williams	535	231.3
5. Gehlbach	Gee Bee R-2	535	222.09
6. Hall	Hall *Bulldog*	535	215.57
7. Ong	Howard *Ike*	160	191.07
	1933		
1. Wedell	Wedell-Williams	535	237.9 mph
2. Gehlbach	Wedell-Williams	535	224.9
3. Minor	Howard *Mike*	225	199.87
4. Hague	Keith Rider R-2	125	183.2
5. Granville	Gee Bee Model Y	450	173.07
	1934		
1. Turner	Wedell-Williams	1000	248.12 mph
2. Minor	Brown Special	300	214.9
3. Worthen	Wedell-Williams	535	208.37
4. Neumann	Howard *Ike*	225	207.06
5. R. D. Rae	Keith Rider R-1	250	205.35
6. Chester	Chester *Jeep*	225	191.59
	1935		
1. Neumann	Howard *Mr. Mulligan*	800	220.19
2. Wittman	Wittman *Bonzo*	435	218.68
3. R. D. Rae	Keith Rider R-1	250	213.94
4. Jacobson	Howard *Mike*	225	209.1
5. Miles	Seversky SEV-3	715	193.59
6. McKeen	Brown Special	250	188.85
Turner	Wedell-Williams	1000	
	1936		
1. Detroyat	Caudron C-460	380	264.26 mph
2. Ortman	Keith Rider R-3	750	248.04
3. R. D. Rae	Keith Rider R-4	250	236.55
4. Neumann	Folkerts *Toots*	225	233.07
5. McKeen	Brown *Miss Los Angeles*	300	230.46
6. Crosby	Crosby Special	300	226.07
	1937		
1. Kling	Folkerts *Jupiter*	400	256.91 mph
2. Ortman	Marcoux-Bromberg (K-R R-3)	800	256.85
3. Turner	Laird-Turner	1000	253.8
4. Sinclair	Seversky SEV-S2	1000	252.36
5. Wittman	Wittman *Bonzo*	485	250.1
6. Moore	Seversky SEV-S2	1000	238.4
7. Gotch	Schoenfeldt *Firecracker*	330	217.8

Pilot	Aircraft	hp	Speed

1938

	Pilot	Aircraft	hp	Speed
1.	Turner	Laird-Turner	1100	283.419 mph
2.	Ortman	Marcoux-Bromberg	900	269.7
3.	Wittman	Wittman *Bonzo*	485	259.1
4.	Wade	HM-1 (formerly *Time Flies*)	900	249.8
5.	Mackey	Wedell-Williams	1000	249.6
6.	Jacobson	Keith Rider *Eight Ball*	400	214.5

1939

	Pilot	Aircraft	hp	Speed
1.	Turner	Laird-Turner	1100	282.5 mph
2.	LeVier	Schoenfeldt *Firecracker*	350	272.5
3.	Ortman	Marcoux-Bromberg	900	254.4
4.	Crosby	Crosby Special CR-4	400	244.5
5.	Wittman	Wittman *Bonzo*	485	241.3
6.	Mackey	Wedell-Williams	1000	232.9

1946

	Pilot	Aircraft	hp	Speed
1.	Johnston	P-39Q *Aircobra*	2000	373.9 mph
2.	LeVier	P-38L-5 *Lightning*	3400	370.1
3.	Ortman	P-51D-30 *Mustang*	2270	367.6
4.	Raymond	P-51D *Mustang*	2270	364.65
5.	Swanson	P-51D *Mustang*	2270	362.05
6.	Cleland	F2G-1 *Corsair*	2400	357.46
7.	Edmundson	P-51D *Mustang*	2270	354.39
8.	Wittman	P-63C-5 *Kingcobra*	1700	341.2
9.	Lilly	P-63A *Kingcobra*	1700	328.15
10.	Pemberton	P-63F *Kingcobra*	1700	304.4

1947

	Pilot	Aircraft	hp	Speed
1.	Cleland	F2G-1 *Corsair*	4000	396.13 mph
2.	Becker	F2G-1 *Corsair*	4000	390.13
3.	Demming	P-39Q *Aircobra*	2000	389.83
4.	Beville	P-51D *Mustang*	2270	360.84
5.	LeVier	P-38L-5 *Lightning*	3400	357.48
6.	Bour	P-63A *Kingcobra*	1700	327.28

1948

	Pilot	Aircraft	hp	Speed
1.	Johnson	P-51D *Mustang*	2270	383.76 mph
2.	Raymond	P-51D *Mustang*	2270	365.23
3.	Newhall	P-63C-5 *Kingcobra*	1700	313.56
	Brown	P-39Q *Aircobra*	out 19th lap at 392.4	

1949

	Pilot	Aircraft	hp	Speed
1.	Cleland	F2G-1 *Corsair*	4000	397.07 mph
2.	Puckett	F2G-1 *Corsair*	4000	393.52
3.	McKillen	F2G-1 *Corsair*	4000	387.58
4.	Beville	P-51D *Mustang*	2270	381.21
5.	Tucker	P-63C-5 *Kingcobra*	2000	378.34
6.	Hagerstrom	P-51D *Mustang*	2270	372.71
7.	Newhall	P-51K *Mustang*	2270	372.32
8.	Hannon	P-51A *Mustang*	1700	300.39
	Johnson	P-51D *Mustang*	2270	
	Odom	P-51C *Mustang*	2270	

Pilot	Aircraft	hp	Speed	

BENDIX TROPHY RACE

1931

	Pilot	Aircraft	hp	Speed	
1.	Doolittle	Laird *Super Solution*	535	223.03	mph
2.	H. Johnson	Lockheed *Orion*	450	198.8	
3.	Blevins	Lockheed *Orion*	450	188.99	
4.	Eaker	Lockheed *Altair*	550	186.07	

1932

	Pilot	Aircraft	hp	Speed	
1.	Haizlip	Wedell-Williams	535	245	mph
2.	Wedell	Wedell-Williams	535	232	
3.	Turner	Wedell-Williams	535	226	
4.	Gehlbach	Gee Bee R-2	535	210	
	Vance	Vance Flying Wing	800		

1933

	Pilot	Aircraft	hp	Speed	
1.	Turner	Wedell-Williams	900	214.78	mph
2.	Wedell	Wedell-Williams	535	209.23	
	Boardman	Gee Bee R-1	800		
	Thaw	Gee Bee R-2	750		
	Gehlbach	Wedell-Williams	535		
	Earhart	Lockheed Vega	450		

1934

	Pilot	Aircraft	hp	Speed	
1.	Davis	Wedell-Williams	535	216.23	mph
2.	Worthen	Wedell-Williams	535	203.21	
	Gehlbach	Gee Bee QED	800		

1935

	Pilot	Aircraft	hp	Speed	
1.	Howard-Israel	Howard *Mr. Mulligan*	800	238.7	mph
2.	Turner	Wedell-Williams	1000	238.5	
3.	Thaw	Northrup *Gamma*	775	201.9	
4.	Hunt	Lockheed *Orion*	535	174.76	

1936

	Pilot	Aircraft	hp	Speed	
1.	Thaden-Noyes	Staggerwing Beech	420	165.3	mph
2.	Ingalls	Lockheed *Orion*	535	157.46	
3.	Bulick	Vultee V1A	735	156.49	
4.	Pomeroy	Douglas DC-2	1470	151.46	
5.	Earhart	Lockheed *Electra*	900	148.72	
	Howard-Wife	Howard *Mr. Mulligan*	800		
	Jacobson	Northrup *Gamma*	775		
	Miles	Gee Bee QED	900		

1937

	Pilot	Aircraft	hp	Speed	
1.	Fuller	Seversky SEV-S2 (P-35)	1000	258.24	mph
2.	Ortman	Marcoux-Bromberg	700	224.83	
3.	Cochran	Staggerwing Beech	450	194.74	
4.	Sinclair	Seversky SEV-S2	1000	184.92	
5.	Burcham	Lockheed 12	900	184.52	
6.	Sundorph	Sundorph A-1	225	166.2	
	Perlick	Staggerwing Beech (A17F)	700		
	Mackey	Wedell-Williams	900		

Pilot	Aircraft	hp	Speed

1938

1. Cochran	Seversky SEV-S2	1200	249.74 mph
2. Fuller	Seversky SEV-S2	1200	238.6
3. Mantz	Lockheed *Orion*	750	206.579
4. Constant	Staggerwing Beech	450	199.33
5. Hadley	Staggerwing Beech	450	181.84
6. LaJatte	Spartan 7W	450	177.4
Armistead	Gee Bee QED	900	
Perlick	Staggerwing Beech (A17F)	700	
Cordova	Bellanca tri-motor (1 Ranger, 2 Menascos)		
Gehlbach	Wedell-Williams	535	

1939

1. Fuller	Seversky SEV-S2	1200	282.09 mph
2. Bussy	Bellanca tri-motor	870	244.48
3. Mantz	Lockheed *Orion*	750	234.87
4. Constant	Staggerwing Beech	450	231.36
5. Arlene Davis	Spartan 7W	450	196.84
6. Maycock	Staggerwing Beech	450	187.18

1946

1. Mantz	P-51C *Mustang*	2270	435.5
2. Cochran	P-5B1 *Mustang*	2270	420.9
3. Mayson	P-51C *Mustang*	2270	408.22
4. Eddy	P-51D *Mustang*	2270	373.25
5. Harp	P-38 *Lightning*	3420	370.44
6. Husted	Douglas A-26C	4000	367.88
7. Tucker	P-63C-5 *Kingcobra*	1710	367.14

1947

1. Mantz	P-51C *Mustang*	2270	460.42 mph
2. DeBona	P-51D *Mustang*	2270	458.2
3. Lunken	P-51D *Mustang*	2270	408.7
4. Gimbel	P-51B *Mustang*	2270	404.08
5. Eddy	P-51D *Mustang*	2270	376.54
6. Mayson	P-51C *Mustang*	2270	376.08
7. Whitton	FG-1 *Corsair*	2000	320.02

1948

1. Mantz	P-51C *Mustang*	2270	447.98 mph
2. Carney	P-51C *Mustang*	2270	446.11
3. Cochran	P-51B *Mustang*	2270	445.84
4. Lunken	P-51D *Mustang*	2270	441.59
5. Stallings	DH *Mosquito*	4540	341.12
DeBona	P-51C *Mustang*	2270	

1949

1. DeBona	P-51C *Mustang*	2270	470.136 mph
2. Reaver	P-51C *Mustang*	2270	450.22
3. Salmon	P-51C *Mustang*	2270	449.21
4. Bussart	DH *Mosquito*	4540	343.75
Cameron	Martin B-26C	4000	
Perron	Republic AT-12	1000	

Pilot	Aircraft	hp	Speed

1934

Greve racers were limited to engines of 550 cu. in. displacement or less. All powerplants were Menasco four-cylinder or six-cylinder in-line air-cooled models or the Cirrus engine of similar design. See text for point system scoring.

Pilot	Aircraft	Speed	
Miles	Miles & Atwood Special	206.24	1st place on points
Chester	Chester *Jeep*	203.38	tie for 2nd on points
R. D. Rae	Keith Rider R-1	211	tie for 2nd on points
Neumann	Howard *Ike*	211.55	3rd place on points
Minor	Brown Special B-2	213.25	4th place on points

1935

Pilot	Aircraft	Speed	
Neumann	Howard *Mike*	212.71	1st on points
R. D. Rae	Keith Rider R-1	210.12	2nd on points
Chester	Chester *Jeep*	199.07	3rd on points
Wittman	*Chief Oshkosh*	189.38	4th on points
McKeen	Brown Special B-2	206.42	5th on points
Miles	Miles & Atwood Special	189.6	6th on points
Elmendorf	Wedell-Williams	175.1	7th on points

1936 (point system discontinued)

Pilot	Aircraft	Speed	
1. Detroyat	Caudron C-460	247.3	mph
2. Neumann	Folkerts *Toots*	225.85	
3. Chester	Chester *Jeep*	224.68	
4. Kling	Keith-Rider *Suzy*	218.33	
5. Jacobson	Howard *Mike*	214.42	
6. R. D. Rae	Keith-Rider R-1	212.32	
7. McKeen	Brown Special B-2	204.47	
Miles	Miles & Atwood Special		

1937

Pilot	Aircraft	Speed	
1. Kling	Folkerts FK-1	232.27	mph
2. Wittman	*Chief Oshkosh*	231.99	
3. Gotch	Schoenfeldt-Rider	231.59	
4. R. D. Rae	Folkerts	224.19	
5. McKeen	Brown B-2	223.64	
6. Haines	Haines H-3	177.71	
7. McArthur	Delgado *Flash*		

1938

Pilot	Aircraft	Speed	
1. LeVier	Schoendfeldt-Rider	250.88	mph
2. Chester	Chester *Goon*	250.41	
3. Jacobson	Rider R-8 *Eightball*	218.27	
4. Ortman	Marcoux-Bromberg	192.5	
5. Crosby	Crosby CR-4		
6. Dory	Bushey-McGrew		

Pilot	Aircraft	hp	Speed

1939

	Pilot	Aircraft		Speed
1.	Chester	Chester *Goon*	263.39	mph
2.	LeVier	Schoendfeldt-Rider		
3.	Crosby	Crosby CR-4		
4.	Williams	Brown B-2		

SOHIO TROPHY RACE

1946

	Pilot	Aircraft	Engine	Speed
1.	Fulton	P-51D *Mustang*	Packard V-1650	352.78 mph
2.	Ong	P-51D *Mustang*	Packard V-1650	345.86
3.	Hardwick	Lockheed F5G	Allison V-1710	322.62
4.	Newhall	P-63 *Kingcobra*	Allison V-1710	310.54
5.	Ortman	Lockheed P-38	Allison V-1710	303.9
6.	DeSanto	Lockheed F5D	Allison V-1710	303.68
7.	Bing	P-39 *Aircobra*	Allison V-1710	**276.1**

1947

Sohio Trophy Race for Lockheed Lightnings only. All engines Allison V-1710.

	Pilot	Speed
1.	LeVier	360.86 mph
2.	Walling	351.78
3.	Hill	347.39
4.	Thomson	328.73
5.	Hlavacek	270.19

Kendall Trophy Race for P-51 Mustangs only. 2nd & 3rd place Allison engines; others Packards.

	Pilot	Speed
1.	Beville	384.6 mph
2.	Everson	377.92
3.	Edmundson	372.39
4.	Fairbrother	367.03
5.	Murray	357.08

Tinnerman Trophy Race for P-63 Kingcobras only. All engines Allison V-1710.

	Pilot	Speed
1.	Knight	352.16 mph
2.	Tucker	347.65
3.	Wittman	339.46
4.	Whiteside	313.51
5.	Bour	254.91

Allison Trophy Race for P-80 jets only. All engines J 33 Allisons.

	Pilot	Speed
1.	Capt. Bernor	494.27
2.	Capt. Bishop	480.42
3.	Col. Schilling	478.22
4.	Capt. Armstrong	471.90
5.	Lt. LaRose	471.52

SOHIO TROPHY RACE, 1948

	Pilot	Aircraft	Handicap	Speed
1.	Eucker	P-63 *Kingcobra*	137.5 sec.	320.22 mph
2.	Gidovlenko	P-38 *Lightning*	1.5 sec.	317.95
3.	Walling	P-51 *Mustang*	180.2 sec.	316.87
4.	Raymond	P-51 *Mustang*	151.8 sec.	315.62
5.	Bing	P-51 *Mustang*	188.3 sec.	312.94
6.	Hardwick	F-5 *Lightning*	86. sec.	312.65
7.	Singer	P-63 *Kingcobra*	none	308.34
8.	Newhall	P-63 *Kingcobra*	101.5 sec.	302.96
9.	Saum	P-38 *Lightning*	disqualified - dangerous flying.	

Pilot	Aircraft	hp	Speed

TINNERMAN TROPHY RACE, 1948

Pilot	Aircraft	Engine	Speed	
1. Raymond	P-51 *Mustang*	Packard V-1650	362.24	mph
2. Eucker	P-63 *Kingcobra*	Allison V-1710	362.09	
3. Newhall	P-63 *Kingcobra*	Allison V-1710	314.12	
Fairbrother	P-51 *Mustang*	Packard V-1650		
Singer	P-63 *Kingcobra*	Allison V-1710		

SOHIO TROPHY RACE, 1949

Pilot	Aircraft	Engine	Speed	
1. Odom	P-51 *Mustang*	Packard V-1650	388.39	mph
2. Puckett	F2G-1 *Corsair*	P. & W. R-4360	384.88	
3. Tucker	P-63 *Kingcobra*	Allison V-1710	381.52	
4. Beville	P-51 *Mustang*	Packard V-1650	376.71	
5. Cooley	P-51 *Mustang*	Packard V-1650	373.43	
6. Singer	P-63 *Kingcobra*	Allison V-1710	359.06	
7. Fairbrother	P-51 *Mustang*	Packard V-1650	349.6	
8. Whiteside	P-63 *Kingcobra*	Allison V-1710	330.35	

TINNERMAN TROPHY RACE, 1949

Pilot	Aircraft	Engine	Speed	
1. McKillen	F2G-1 *Corsair*	P&WR 4360	386.06	mph
2. Newhall	P-51 *Mustang*	Packard V-1650	379.73	
3. McArthur	XIV *Spitfire*	Rolls Griffin	359.56	
4. Hardwick	F-5 *Lightning*	Allison V-1710	328.47	
5. Hagerstrom	P-38 *Lightning*	Allison V-1710	311.59	
Hannon	P-51 *Mustang*	Allison V-1710		
Gidovlenko	P-38 *Lightning*	Allison V-1710		

GOODYEAR TROPHY RACE, 1947
(All Goodyear Racers powered with Continental C-85)

1. Bill Brennand	Wittman *Buster*	165.857	mph
2. Paul Penrose	Chester *Swee' Pea*	165.393	
3. Fish Salmon	Cosmic Wind Special	158.798	
4. Tony LeVier	Cosmic Wind *Little Toni*	157.851	
5. Warren Siem	*Loose Siem*	151.270	
6. B. F. Robinson	Modified Brown Special	143.865	

GOODYEAR TROPHY RACE, 1948

1. Fish Salmon	Cosmic Wind *Minnow*	169.688
2. Steve Wittman	Wittman Special	168.862
3. Art Chester	Chester *Swee' Pea II*	168.201
4. Bill Brennand	Wittman *Buster*	167.063
5. B. F. Robinson	Cosmic Wind *Little Toni*	165.106
6. P. C. Quigley	Pitts Special	164.892
7. R. B. Downey	Cosmic Wind *Ballerina*	161.453
8. M. L. LeFevers	Falcon Special	156.584

Pilot	Aircraft	Speed

GOODYEAR TROPHY RACE, 1949

1. Bill Brennand	Wittman *Buster*	177.340	mph
2. Keith Sorensen	*Deerfly*	176.726	
3. Steve Wittman	Wittman *Bonzo*	176.244	
4. Vincent Ast	Cosmic Wind *Ballerina*	175.974	
5. Fish Salmon	Cosmic Wind *Minnow*	175.728	
6. Cliff Mone	Williams *Estrellita*	175.016	
7. Bob Downey	Mercury Air	171.359	
8. Luther Johnson	Long LA-1	167.308	
9. James Kistler	Kistler Special	153.369	
Al Foss	*Jinny*		

CONTINENTAL MOTORS RACE
(All engines Continental C-85)

1948 at Miami

1. Bill Brennand	Wittman Special	166.473	mph
2. Fish Salmon	Cosmic Wind *Minnow*	158.532	
3. Art Chester	Chester *Swee' Pea*	145.650	
4. Earl Ortman	Loose Special	127.339	

1949 at Miami

1. Steve Wittman	Wittman *Bonzo*	176.867
2. Bill Brennand	Wittman *Buster*	174.193
3. T. B. Heisel	Pitts Special	170.011
4. Dave Long	Long *Peashooter*	166.763

1950 at Miami

1. Steve Wittman	Wittman *Bonzo*	185.400
2. Keith Sorensen	Cosmic Wind *Ballerina*	182.044
3. Bob Downey	*Shoestring*	181.334
4. Phil Quigley	Pitts *Li'l Monster*	175.885

1950 at Detroit

1. John Jones	Cosmic Wind *Little Toni*	187.785
2. Steve Wittman	Wittman *Bonzo*	185.050
3. Keith Sorensen	*Deerfly*	184.576
4. Kip Mone	Williams *Estrellita*	181.971

1951 at Detroit

1. John Jones	*Shoestring*	197.218
2. Steve Wittman	Wittman *Bonzo*	192.174
3. Keith Sorensen	Modified Foss *Little Mike*	187.476
4. Bill Brennand	Pitts *Li'l Monster*	187.053

1952 at Detroit

1. Steve Wittman	Wittman *Bonzo*	197.29
2. Bill Falck	Falck *Rivets*	194.38
3. Bill Brennand	Pitts Special II	192.31
4. Bob Porter	Wittman *Buster*	180.72
5. Jim Kistler	Kistler *Skeeter*	
6. John P. Jones	*Shoestring*	

Pilot	Aircraft	Speed

SAN DIEGO, CALIFORNIA, April 24, 1949

1. Fish Salmon	Cosmic Wind *Minnow*	175.27
2. Steve Wittman	Wittman *Bonzo*	175
3. Bob Downey	Cosmic Wind *Ballerina*	174
4. Bill Brennand	Wittman *Buster*	171
5. Bill Broadbeck	Chester *Skybaby*	

(note: Bob Heisel (Pitts *Pellet*) killed during first heat. In second heat, Art Chester *(Swee' Pea II)* killed).

NEWHALL, CALIFORNIA, May 8, 1949

1. Bob Downey	Cosmic Wind *Minnow*	169.4
2. Steve Wittman	Wittman *Bonzo*	163.3
3. Bill Brennand	Wittman *Buster*	159
5. Bill Broadbeck	Chester *Skybaby*	158.6
5. Billie Robinson	Cosmic Wind *Little Toni*	154.2

ONTARIO, CALIFORNIA, May 22. 1949

1. Bob Downey	Cosmic Wind *Minnow*	176
2. Steve Wittman	Wittman *Bonzo*	171.8
3. Billie Robinson	Cosmic Wind *Little Toni*	171
4. Bill Brennand	Wittman *Buster*	170.6
5. Keith Sorensen	*Deerfly*	169

WHITE PLAINS, N. Y., June 24, 1950

1. Bill Brennand	Wittman *Buster*	175.97
2. Luther Johnson	Long Midget	161.12
3. Jim Miller	Miller *Little Gem*	158.53
4. Steve Wittman	Wittman *Bonzo*	
5. Bart Denight	Denight Special	

SAN JOSE, CALIFORNIA, June 25, 1950

1. Vincent Ast	*Shoestring*	175
2. Bob Downey	Cosmic Wind *Ballerina*	174.3
3. Eddie Custer	Cosmic Wind *Minnow*	174
4. John P. Jones	Cosmic Wind *Little Toni*	173
5. Jim Kistler	Kistler *Skeeter*	160.5

CHATTANOOGA, TENNESSEE, July 16, 1950

1. Bill Brennand	Wittman *Buster*	176.69
2. Phil Quigley	Pitts Special II	175.86
3. Jimmy Wilson	Pack *Li'l Rebel*	163.02
4. Art Beckington	Parks Alumni Special*	158.17

* *Pusher-type*

Pilot	*Aircraft*	*hp*	*Speed*

READING, PENNSYLVANIA, Sept. 24, 1950 (REBAT TROPHY)

1. Steve Wittman	Wittman *Bonzo*		185.57
2. Bill Brennand	Wittman *Buster*		183.71
3. Phil Quigley	Pitts Special II		179.25
4. Jim Miller	Miller *Little Gem*		169.55
5. Bart Denight	Denight Special		167.77
6. Bill Falck	Falck *Rivets*		167.09

CHATTANOOGA, TENNESSEE, May 20, 1951

1. Steve Wittman	Wittman *Bonzo*		178.36
2. Bob Downey	Cosmic Wind *Minnow*		176.32
3. Jim Wilson	Pack *Li'l Rebel*		165.86
4. Bob Porter	Wittman *Buster*		165.64
5. Joe Mangano	Pack *Johnny Reb*		

READING, PENNSYLVANIA, August 12, 1951 (REBAT TROPHY)

1. Steve Wittman	Wittman *Bonzo*		184.69
2. Bob Porter	Wittman *Buster*		180.68
3. Jim Wilson	Pack *Li'l Rebel*		179.18
4. Luther Johnson	Long Midget		169.55
5. Bill Brennand	Pitts Special II		164.45

CHATTANOOGA, TENNESSEE, May 18, 1952

1. Bill Falck	Falck *Rivets*		186.95
2. Steve Wittman	Wittman *Bonzo*		186.79
3. Bob Porter	Wittman *Buster*		176.91
4. Bill Brennand	Pitts Special II		175.97
5. Jim Wilson	Pack *Li'l Rebel*		174.60

(No races in 1953)

DANSVILLE, N.Y., July 4, 1954

1. Jim Miller	Miller *Little Gem*		181.06
2. Dick Ohm	*Shoestring*		180.94
3. Bob Porter	Wittman *Buster*		176.33
4. Phil Quigley	*Mammy*		166.6
5. Bart Denight	Denight Special		166.09

DANSVILLE, N.Y., July 3, 1955, (Frank E. Gannett Trophy)

1. Bill Falck	Falck *Rivets*		186.85
2. Steve Wittman	Wittman *Bonzo*		185.33
3. Dick Ohm	*Shoestring*		181.82
4. Tom Cassutt	Cassutt Special		180.68
5. John Scoville	Scoville *Stardust*		157.26

SPRINGFIELD, ILLINOIS, May 27, 1956

1. Bill Falck	Falck *Rivets*		191.07
2. Steve Wittman	Wittman *Bonzo*		190.02
3. Tom Cassutt	Cassutt Special		188.77
4. Marion Cole	*Tater Chip*		165.26
5. Mel Stickney	*Mammy*		

Pilot	Aircraft	hp	Speed

NIAGARA FALLS, N.Y., July 8, 1956 (Frank E. Gannett Trophy)

1. Bill Falck	Falck *Rivets*		199.96
2. Steve Wittman	Wittman *Bonzo*		199.15
3. Tom Cassutt	Cassutt Special		197.62
4. Marion Cole	*Shoestring*		191.42
5. Charlie Bishop	Pack *Li'l Rebel*		163.09

(Note: Scoville crashed in first heat).

OSHKOSH, WISCONSIN, August 5, 1956 (S. J. WITTMAN TROPHY)

1. Steve Wittman	Wittman *Bonzo*		196.84
2. Bill Falck	Falck *Rivets*		196.72
3. Dick Ohm	*Shoestring*		188.45
4. Charlie Bishop	Pack *Johnny Reb*		178.19

OSHKOSH, WISCONSIN, August 11, 1957 (S. J. Wittman Trophy)

1. Steve Wittman	Wittman *Bonzo*		192.76
2. Tom Cassutt	Cassutt Special		187.04
3. Bill Falck	Falck *Rivets*		186.39
4. Dick Ohm	*Shoestring*		179.91
5. Don Tygert	Ohm Special		172.21

FORT WAYNE, INDIANA, September 1, 1957

1. Bill Falck	Falck *Rivets*		196.65
2. Steve Wittman	Wittman *Bonzo*		196.29
3. Tom Cassutt	Cassutt Special		191.42
4. Charlie Bishop	Pack *Johnny Reb*		187.18
5. Dick Ohm	*Shoestring*		187.14
6. Jim Miller	Miller *Little Gem*		175.98

FULTON, N.Y., July 6, 1958

1. Bill Falck	Falck *Rivets*		196.72
2. Tom Cassutt	Cassutt Special		196.19
3. Steve Wittman	Wittman *Bonzo*		192.24
4. Don Tygert	*Shoestring*		189.27

FORT WAYNE, INDIANA. Aug. 31, 1958 (Ft. Wayne Industries Trophy)

1. Tom Cassutt	Cassutt Special		195.8
2. Steve Wittman	Wittman *Bonzo*		193.9
3. Bill Falck	Falck *Rivets*		193.15
4. Jim Miller	Miller *Little Gem*		190.78
5. Mel Stickney	Pack *Li'l Rebel*		188.6
6. Charlie Bishop	Pack *Johnny Reb*		183.99

FORT WAYNE, INDIANA, September 20, 1959

1. Jim Miller	Miller *Little Gem*		199.15
2. Bill Falck	Falck *Rivets*		196.94
3. Paul Booth	Pack *Grey Ghost*		188.49
4. Tom Cassutt	Cassutt Special II		182.12
5. Charlie Bishop	Pack *Johnny Reb*		181.5
6. Mel Stickney	*Shoestring*		177.73

140

Pilot	Aircraft	hp	Speed

FORT WAYNE, INDIANA, July 4, 1960

1. Jim Miller	Miller *Little Gem*		200.23
2. Bill Falck	Falck *Rivets*		198.89
3. John Thomson	*Jersey Skeeter*		195.5
4. Steve Wittman	Wittman *Bonzo*		194.67
5. Jan Christie	Cassutt Special II		193.73
6. Mel Stickney	*Deerfly*		187.82